Red and White

THE WINE APPRECIATION GUILD
San Francisco

For Sophie

and

For Adair

Red and White

photography Adrian Lander

updated edition

wine made simple Max Allen

Published in North America by
The Wine Appreciation Guild
360 Swift Avenue
South San Francisco, CA 94080
800 231-9463
Fax 650 866-3513
www.wineappreciation.com

New Revised Edition published
in 2001 by The Wine Appreciation Guild

ISBN 1 891267-37-X

Designed by Andrew Cunningham and Luisa Laino
Typeset by Luisa Laino
Printed in Malaysia by Times Offset (M) Sdn. Bhd.

Foreword

I was asked by the publisher of this book whether I was prepared to read the manuscript from what might loosely be called a technical viewpoint. I agreed because I both like and respect Max Allen, and expected my task would not be at all onerous.

Having picked up the manuscript, I found that I could not put it down. This celebration of wine fired my imagination and caught my attention like no other wine book I have ever read. I was fairly busy at the time, and all sorts of things were pushed to one side as I continued to read the manuscript from start to finish.

I found almost nothing to comment on from the technical side, or for that matter from any critical viewpoint. For this book is as close to perfection as any introduction to wine is ever likely to be. It is beautifully written in a semi-colloquial style; you can almost hear Max talking to you aloud. Yet it is deceptive; the ideas flow clearly and effortlessly, but every word has been chosen with care.

Thus Max achieves the near impossible, simultaneously taking the piss out of wine yet paying homage to it; demystifying it yet exploring and explaining every facet of it. I read the manuscript so avidly because it fascinated and exhilarated me, and I reckon I own more books on wine than most wine lovers will read in a lifetime.

Red and White: Wine Made Simple is in fact a book for beginner and expert alike. It will make you want to rush down to your cellar or local bottle shop, open the very best bottle you can find, and slosh it down. When you do, make sure to take time to toast the best first book ever written by a new author. Next please.

James Halliday

Contents

*This is a new look at a very old subject, a modern taste of
an ancient liquid. It gives you, the reader, a feeling that
you can smell, savour and enjoy the subject while
learning a little bit more about it.*

Introduction

This book is about the fundamentals of wine: what it is, how it's made, and how to enjoy it. It covers the areas that new wine drinkers are always keen to know about, from the grape varieties and what they taste like, through how the different styles of wine are made, to tasting wine, and how moderate wine drinking can help you live longer.

This is not an encyclopedia, or an atlas, or a buying guide. No vintage charts are to be found here, no star ratings, no scoring systems, no graphs, no diagrams, no maps. There are plenty of encyclopedias and atlases and buying guides that will give you all that information and more.

This book has been written for a new generation of Australian wine drinkers, who are just getting into wine and who want to know the basics. But even though it looks at wine from an Australian perspective, it's not just about Australian wine — it's about all wine, so it will make sense to all new wine drinkers, whether they're reading in Melbourne or Manchester, Darwin or Dublin, Sydney or San Francisco. It's not a guide to Australian wine as such, but an Australian guide to wine.

This is a new look at a very old subject, a modern taste of an ancient liquid. It gives you, the reader, a feeling that you can smell, savour and enjoy the subject while learning a little bit more about it. Our aim as we wrote and snapped away furiously was always to take you inside the glass, to immerse you in the atmosphere of the winery or vineyard, to make the wine live for you. We feel that understanding wine more will help you enjoy it more.

This book was first published in 1997, and a few things have changed in the world of wine since then. So we have revised and updated this edition to make sure that you can continue to get the most out of every bottle.

Max Allen & Adrian Lander

Wine is …

Wine is everywhere. It's on countless tables next to countless lovingly cooked meals; it's out there quenching thirsts at a thousand barbecues; it is written about in detail in magazines and newspapers; it's on shelf after shelf after shelf after shelf. We are very lucky people. Wine in the twenty-first century is as much a part of popular culture as music, TV, sport or food — especially food — but it hasn't always been this way. For thousands of years wine existed at opposite ends of the social spectrum — consumed in great quantity as rough-as-guts plonk by millions of workers and peasants in the countries that produced it, and shrouded in mystery and elitism by the upper-classes of the countries that imported it. Today, wine is neither something to be endured nor something to be exalted. It's just *there*, everywhere, available and accessible to everybody.

The old bloke's been coming to the pub every day after work for thirty years. He works at the big winery up the road. This is wine country and most of the people in this small South Australian town are involved with wine in some way or another, either as growers or, like the old man here, in one of the many wineries. Some of these wineries look more like refineries, and employ hundreds of people.

Today's been particularly hot and dusty, and the old bloke's glad to be in the cool pub as he takes his usual seat at the end of the weathered bar and nods to all the familiar faces. The bartender takes a bottle of port from the fridge and pours a frosty beer glass full to the brim, like he does every day. He hands it to the old man, who takes a grateful mouthful. There was a time the only kinds of alcohol this bar stocked were beer, spirits and fortified wines like this port. Now there's sparkling wine in the fridge too, and chardonnay, and dozens of different wines in the bottle shop next door. Not that the old bloke's tried any of them. He'll stick to his chilled port, thanks very much.

Wine is big business. The world trade in wine could keep a small nation afloat for a year. Hundreds of thousands of people across the globe rely on growing grapes, fermenting them and selling the resulting wine for their livelihood. Australia produces roughly 700 million litres of the stuff every year, yet this is only about two per cent of a world production of 28 billion litres. That's an awful lot of wine. But even when the wine industry seems like exactly that — just another industry — you can always find the romance at its heart. Owning a vineyard can be like frantically stuffing millions of dollar coins into a long concrete pipe and ten years later seeing one dollar squeeze out the other end. But still people give up their day jobs, head out into the bush, plant vines and join the legion of those who have gone before, trying to make the best wine they can. It's as though they're under a spell.

Beads of sweat appear on the auctioneer's forehead. He's got two strong bidders in the room, both very keen to get their hands on lot 95: twelve bottles of forty-year-old Australian shiraz, in perfect condition in their original timber case. This wine is recognised by the world wine media as the finest example of its kind, and each of these bidders, both serious collectors, would love to have this case stashed away in their cellar.

The latest bid has just nudged past the highest price previously paid for this wine. The auctioneer calls out, asking whether it's the last. The tension and heat in the room are almost overwhelming. The sums involved run to five figures. One hundred eyes watch the two bidders as one frets over whether to push the price further still. He does and the crowd lets out a gasp. The other bidder shakes his head and the auctioneer knows it's over. The hammer comes down and everyone breathes again.

The auctioneer briefly wonders whether those twelve bottles will ever be drunk. It's far more likely that the case won't be opened and the collector will sit on it for a few more years until the value goes up even further. What a shame, he thinks. He drank a bottle of the same wine just last year and although it tasted extraordinary, it was certainly fading and tasted old. When this case is opened, he thinks, it might well be too late to enjoy the contents.

Wine is magic. The fact that something as disarmingly humble as fermented grape juice can give me as much pleasure as the most complex, passionately performed music, can take me on journeys as illuminating as any trek into the wilderness, can make me feel better than any pills and can taste better than the most brilliantly cooked meal never ceases to amaze me. No wonder wine has such a strong historical association with the gods — to ancient minds, a naturally produced elixir that not only tasted good but also had such pleasurable mind-altering, mood-enhancing effects just had to come from some Other World, didn't it? From Bacchus, the pink-fleshed, wine-stained, ancient god of indulgence, lolling like a beached whale in a vat of sticky grapes, to the ever-so-serious concept of the blood of Christ, wine has lubricated Western civilisations for centuries. And healed them, too.

She never really drank wine when she was younger, even though her parents did. Her dad had a cellar, and she remembered endless family holidays driving past vineyards and standing around in winery tasting rooms getting bored.

Then she left school, went to uni, and discovered cask wine for herself. She drank this quite happily until one day, wandering through the local wine shop, she was offered a tasting of some expensive wine from a local winery that she'd never dream of buying. What the hell, the tasting was free.

This was unlike anything she'd experienced before. The wine was delicious, mesmerising, magical. She was hooked, and two weeks later she found herself driving out to the winery in the rain. She pulled in to the small car park and squeezed her battered old Datsun between two brand-new BMWs.

Inside she waited as a group of well-dressed older people waffled on to each other about the nuances of the wines on tasting, talking in jargon she didn't understand. And she couldn't believe it when these people left, complaining under their breath that the prices were too high.

Maybe the wine she'd tasted in the bottle shop wasn't really that good? After all, what would she know? Nervously she took a sip from the glass handed to her over the counter. There it was, that same haunting flavour. She handed over the dollars she'd been saving all week and left the winery, clutching her bottle. And she went home, invited her boyfriend over and together they drank every last drop.

Wine is for drinking. Never forget this. Put wine on your table. Have it there at mealtimes. Let your children taste it. Ignore what you read in this book and other books, and break all the rules if you want to. Drink big reds from mugs. Put ice in fresh young whites when the weather's really hot. Experiment. Drink red wine with white fish and white wine with red meat — it might taste disgusting, but then again, it might taste wonderful. Try everything at least once. Get obsessed. Build a cellar under the house, go to wine tastings, buy your wine from a winery, read all the books, learn all the jargon, spend lots of money. But drink the most expensive champagne with fish and chips on the beach. Open the most expensive red at a barbecue. Drink wine every day. That's what it's for. Wine is for drinking. Wine is good for you.

I can still remember the taste of the first wine that really caught me in its spell. I'd just finished art school in England, where I drank wine occasionally but was far more interested in beer. I had come to Australia to visit family, and one weekend a friend drove us out to the nearest wine region. It was a hot, two-hour journey, and everyone was cranky by the time we got to the first winery. I don't even think I really wanted to be there, but I tried the glass of shiraz that was handed to me all the same.

It was as though somebody had opened a door to another world and invited me in. This glass was overflowing with smells of deep dark fruit and roasting coffee and licorice and . . . and the taste! This was nothing like the cheap French plonk I was used to. If this is what wine could be like then I wanted more.

When I got back to England, I went on the dole. But unlike the millions of other unemployed people, I would collect my dole money, dash to the nearest wine shop, and spend most of it on the best wines I could find.

I sold my possessions to buy wine books. I ate baked beans so that I could afford good wine glasses. Wine was an obsession, and very soon I needed more money to fund my habit. So I got a job in a wine shop. And while I was there I fell in love with an Australian woman, who has brought me back to where it had all started. Now, as a wine writer, I have the enviable job of writing about something I love — writing about my obsession.

And I hope my words might open the same door for a few other people, and infect them with the passion for wine that's given me so much pleasure over the last few years.

Vineyard

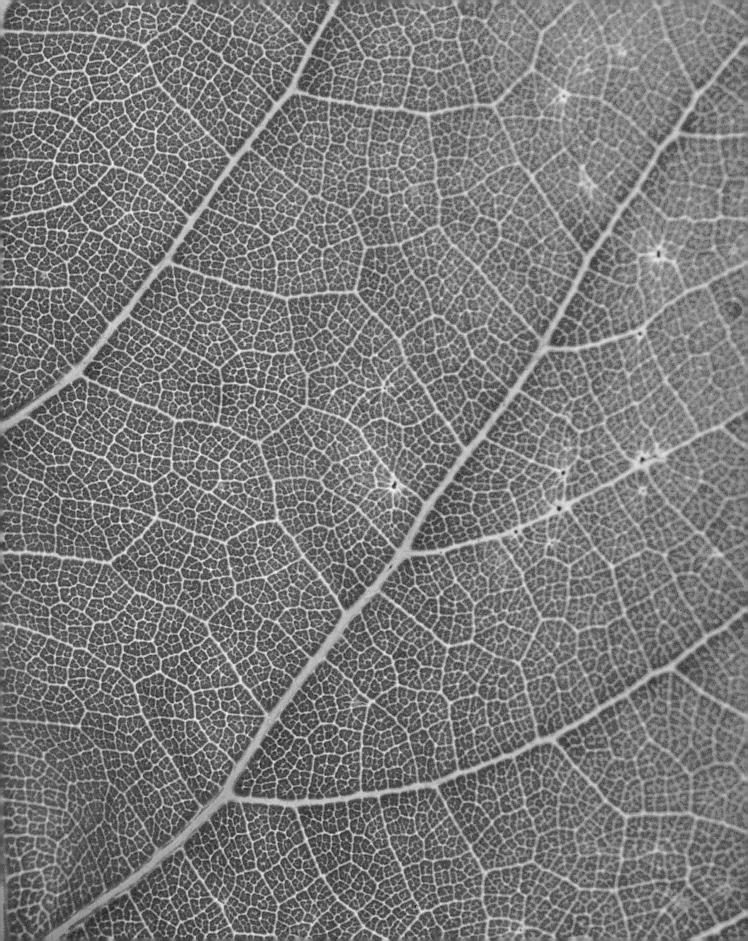

The Flavours of Wine

Wine is the best convenience food in the world.
It's all there in the bottle, just waiting to be enjoyed.
You don't have to heat it, or mix it with anything, or
garnish it, or chop it up or bung it in a wok. All you
have to do is pull the cork and put it in a glass. Simple.
Everything that can be done to make the drinking experience
as enjoyable as possible has been done for you before you buy a bottle
(apart from perhaps sticking it in a fridge to cool down). A long chain of
events stretches back through the cork and into the wine shop, through
warehouses, out of the city and into the country, through the winery,
through tanks, barrels and crushers into baskets, through pickers' hands
into grapes and right back through the vine to the sun and the rain and
the earth.

It always starts out there. Wine drinking is done mostly in an urban
environment, but winemaking is always done in the country —
sometimes rugged, sometimes genteel, but almost always beautiful
country. To understand a little more about where the different flavours in
wine come from, it helps if you understand about grapes and vines and
vineyards and wineries. Short of actually getting out there and tramping
around vineyards, getting mud on your boots and dirt on your hands, a
quick browse through the following pages might help you come closer to
that understanding.

You can't make a silk purse out of a sow's ear. I've always loved that expression. It's so medieval or something. So visceral.

And it's an expression that applies beautifully to winemaking, because no matter how hard you try, you can't make good wine out of bad grapes. Common sense really, but you'd be surprised how many people have ignored this plain truth in the past.

Luckily, winemakers have finally admitted that they can have all the brand-spanking-new, shiny stainless-steel equipment and the most expensive barrels and the cleanest winery, but if they are working with less-than-brilliant fruit, they'll make less-than-brilliant wine. So all the attention has turned to the vineyard and getting the grapes right in the first place. Growing the best fruit possible has become the major preoccupation of wine producers in the twenty-first century. They're all out there, right now, playing with the soil and vines, chanting the adage 'wine is made in the vineyard' like a mantra.

The vineyard is where a wine's real flavour comes from. The grape variety used, where the vine is grown, the soil it's in, how the vine is grown, how much sunshine it gets, how much water, when it's picked — all these factors affect the potential flavours, the flavours that can be released from the fruit when it goes to the winery. The winery is where the wine's style is decided, depending on the methods and techniques used by the winemaker.

But let's not get ahead of ourselves. Let's first take a look at each of the elements influencing flavour, starting with the grape varieties, because they probably have the most say in how your wine tastes.

One of the best things to happen to wine in the last two thousand years is the very recent practice of putting the name of the grape variety — or varieties, if the wine is a blend — on the label in big letters. There's no mystery to grape varieties. They're like any other type of fruit or vegetable — different strains, types, mutations, clones give you different flavours. You wouldn't expect a Granny Smith apple to taste like a Red Delicious any more than you'd expect chardonnay to taste like shiraz. So, once you become used to the typical flavours of each variety, choosing the wines you'll like, and having fair expectations about how those wines will taste, becomes a doddle.

White

About white grapes

Chardonnay

God I love chardonnay. No, I mean I really *love* chardonnay. And I'm not the only one: everybody loves chardonnay. Chardonnay grapes are the darlings of the wine world.

Grape growers love the chardonnay vine because it's easy to grow almost anywhere, and, because it's so popular, the farmers can get a good price per tonne for their harvest.

Winemakers love chardonnay because it's one of the most flexible, malleable varieties available to them. Chardonnay grapes, once they're in the winery, can be made into a huge variety of different styles, from crisp, light fizz, through to rich and complex, barrel-fermented, full-bodied dry whites.

And wine drinkers absolutely fall over themselves to drink chardonnay because its flavours are usually so immediate, generous and downright delicious. In other words, wines made from chardonnay grapes are easy to understand. User-friendly.

Once upon a time, not so long ago, nobody had heard of chardonnay. (Yes, I know, almost impossible to believe, but true.) As recently as thirty years ago, the dominant grape variety used for quality white wine in Australia was riesling, and there was only a handful of chardonnay vines in the ground. If you asked a winemaker what chardonnay tasted like then, he (and in those days they *were* all 'he') probably would have had a hard job describing it to you.

You see, for some reason, when wine-making seeped out of the Old World and into the colonies two, three hundred years ago, chardonnay was not one of the grapes the new winemakers took with them. Even though it's the grape responsible for two of France's greatest wine styles (whites from Burgundy and, blended with pinot noir and pinot meunier, the sparkling wines of Champagne), nobody made the connection and thought to try chardonnay in New World soil.

It took until the early 1970s for chardonnay to appear in commercial quantities in Australia — a decade after it had taken off in California and a few years before it hit the ground in New Zealand. But once Australians had tried it, we were hooked. Today the world is in the grip of a chardonnay frenzy — growers are planting it, winemakers are making it and drinkers are drinking it *everywhere*.

Chardonnay has become the Coke of wine. You know how you can be travelling through the remotest outback or quietest village and almost always come across a Coke machine? Well, no matter where you go in the world — Moldova, Bhutan, Uruguay or England — somebody has planted chardonnay and is making a pleasant, slightly peachy, slightly toasty dry white wine out of it.

But that's not the chardonnay I really love. I like it and I'll drink it, and so would most of us, but I'd rather search out a chardonnay from one of the areas in the world that has been proven to make it really, *really* well. I'd rather try a good chardonnay from Burgundy in France or Margaret River or the Adelaide Hills in Australia, or the Napa Valley in California, and revel in the complexities of a great dry white. I want to find a whole spectrum of flavours, depending on the winemaking, ranging from lemon, green apples and grapefruit in unwooded or lightly wooded styles, through melon, peach and cashew in the medium-bodied wines, to toast, butter, fig and honey in the bigger, barrel-fermented and barrel-aged styles. Then I'm happy.

Sauvignon Blanc

'Eeurgh! What the bloody hell's that?'
'That's a glass of good sauvignon blanc.'
'Yuk! It smells like some mangy old cat just pissed on a tomato bush!'
'Yeah. Wonderful, isn't it?'

When it's really good, and drunk while still fresh, (in the first two years after being bottled) sauvignon blanc can split people into those who adore the uncompromising smells and flavours, and those who can't stand them.

The split starts when the grape's on the vine. Unlike chardonnay, which actually tastes fairly bland if you munch on grapes in the vineyard, and needs to be fermented and mucked around with in the winery and perhaps aged for a while in bottle to achieve complexity, most of the distinctive characters of sauvignon blanc are there in the berries when they're picked, and it's just a matter of catching those flavours during the winemaking. Crunch through the dusty skin of a pale green sauvignon blanc grape plucked from a shady vine canopy on a hot day, and your mouth explodes with all the flavours you'd expect to find in the drink.

When sauvignon blanc is good, its flavours can range from fresh-cut grass, asparagus and gooseberry, through the more pungent aromas described above, right into passionfruit and other tropical goodies — even feral, animal flavours akin to sweaty armpits (rare, but delicious. Honest.) When it's good, sauvignon blanc should also have the most refreshingly juicy, crisp acidity and tongue-tingling liveliness, managing to combine intense fruit flavours with sometimes flinty, pebbly dryness.

I know. It's a classic case of the wine writer crapping on about bizarre flavours long after the sensible people have just drunk the wine, but good sauvignon blanc gets me every time: it makes my mouth water.

It has to be *good* though, or sauvignon blanc can be a rather drab drink. Too often it is planted in warmer regions where it loses its essential zinginess and becomes just another faintly fruity, rather flabby white wine. You need an element of coolness about your vineyard's climate to produce balanced sauvignon blanc grapes and good wine. That's why the best regions for the variety are places like Marlborough in New Zealand's South Island, the Adelaide Hills in Australia and the Loire Valley in western France — all areas with a definite chill about them. Look for those names on the label and you'll seldom be disappointed.

'Eeurgh! What the bloody hell's that?'

'That's a glass of good sauvignon blanc.'

'Yuk! It smells like some mangy old cat just pissed on a tomato bush!'

'Yeah. Wonderful, isn't it?'

Sauvignon blanc doesn't only shine on its own. When it's blended with semillon, for example, the flavours of the two grapes complement each other beautifully, the lean grassiness of the one filled out by the fuller juiciness of the other. Sauvignon/semillon blends are gaining popularity in Australia, where they are often produced in fresh, clean, unwooded styles that match food so well. However, sometimes they are spiced up with some fermentation and/or ageing in barrel to produce wines modelled after the whites of Bordeaux: dry, with a hint of greenness and a lick of toasty oak flavour.

Semillon

Sometimes I shock myself. There I am, trotting along thinking that, hey, I'm pretty open-minded and forward-thinking and progressive, then I catch myself saying the kind of things I'd expect my grandfather to say — if he drank wine, that is, which he doesn't.

When it comes to semillon, I catch myself more often than usual, because one of the best things about this grape might go unrealised by future generations of wine drinkers unless some conscientious soul alerts them to it (see what I mean?).

Although wines made from semillon start out fairly neutral-tasting, when grown in certain areas (the warm, wet Hunter Valley in Australia), picked at a certain ripeness (not too ripe, even quite green), and made in a certain way (simply, without any contact with oak barrels), they can age over ten, twenty years into some of the most remarkable, unique and complex white wines in the world.

But semillon *also* lends itself to being picked riper, perhaps aged in barrel to spice it up a bit, put onto the market a year after harvest and guzzled down with great enjoyment before you've had time to blink. The attraction of this riper, drink-now style of semillon is its juicy, lemony flavours, and quite full texture in the mouth — which is why it blends so well with sauvignon blanc, and is mostly used to lift and fill out lean-flavoured chardonnay right across the country (forming the ubiquitous semillon/chardonnay blend).

So, as a wine producer, you're faced with two possibilities. Grow and make something that will sell out fast and will make you lots of cash quickly, or grow and make something that either you or your customers will have to hang on to for years to fully appreciate. Unfortunately, most wine producers are economic rationalists, and usually plump for the first option. (There is another option: let the semillon grapes become infected with the noble rot, botrytis, and make them into a deliciously sweet, dessert style of wine.)

Now you can see that this is where I turn into the boring old drunk in the corner, crying into his beer, bemoaning the fact that nobody's upholding the old traditions any more, whingeing that today's drinkers are just out for a quick fix of fruitiness, trying to convince you that casinos and Pay TV will ruin us all. Luckily, a few souls are still making semillon in the traditional style, and releasing older wines onto the market, so things aren't all bad. But watch out. Unless we keep buying and drinking these, the classic, bottle-aged style will disappear, and the glories of oily, toasty, rich old semillon may be lost to the world forever.

Riesling

Don't read this bit. If you do, you might be tempted to try a glass of good riesling, and if you do *that* then you might get a taste for it, and if you do that then you might start buying it, and that's the *last* thing we need because then riesling will become popular again and winemakers will start charging more for it and that would be a *disaster*.

At the moment riesling is cheap in comparison to the much trendier chardonnay or sauvignon blanc, because riesling suffers from an acute image problem.

People have taken riesling's name in vain once too often. In the past, Australian winemakers used to call all number of different grapes 'riesling' because they were lazy. To add insult to injury, winemakers then began using the name *riesling* as a generic term for cheap, slightly fruity white wine. So, to distinguish the true riesling grape, it was called '*rhine* riesling', a nod to the variety's origins on the banks of the Rhine River in Germany.

To make matters worse, the German winemakers went on a bit of a winemaking holiday during the 1970s and '80s, churning out seas of cheap, sweet wines that did no favours for riesling's noble reputation. Some of the top producers in Germany are once again making some really exciting wines, and the law has changed in Australia, stopping the generic use of the riesling name, but I reckon some people are still confused.

Right, ignore all that, and let's start from scratch. From this point on, and throughout this book, when I say 'riesling', I mean the real thing: the noble white grape variety and nothing else. Okay? Good.

And this is what you can expect from a bottle of good riesling. Dryness, for a start. Because of the misuse of the name on cheap casks of fruity sweet stuff, a lot of people still expect all riesling to be sweet. It *can* be made into luscious, expensive sticky whites, and a good, slightly sweet German riesling is a joy to behold, but most good New World riesling — and great, fuller-bodied riesling from Alsace in France — is dry. Limey, floral, packed with aromatic fruit and lively, juicy flavours, but *dry*.

Riesling is an early-ripening variety, which means it's suited to cooler areas like Germany, Alsace, and the Great Southern region in Western Australia, where it doesn't need so much sun to get lots of flavour. But it has also done very well in the slightly warmer regions of the Clare Valley and hills above the Barossa Valley in South Australia.

It is almost never put into oak barrels, and can be one of the most delicious and rewarding white wines of all. But don't tell anyone, or they'll all want to try some.

Gewürztraminer

If riesling is a bit of a misfit in many people's eyes then gewürztraminer is a downright outcast. But then gewürztraminer has only got itself to blame: its biggest asset is its undoing.

Gewürztraminer is just so bloody obvious. Open a bottle of gewürztraminer and you'll see what I mean. There's this unmistakable aroma and flavour of lychees and rose water — it's a dead give-away. The problem is that, because it's so obvious and the grape lends itself so

readily to being made in a semi-sweet or fully sweet style, that's exactly what most Australian winemakers have done, often blending it with riesling (the ubiquitous traminer/riesling is one of the great success stories in popularising Australian wine).

But it has also irreversibly fixed gewürztraminer in the minds of many drinkers as a sweet grape variety. The fact is that gewürztraminer makes a stunning dry white wine, too, but there is very little demand for it.

When it's made well (by the few Australian producers who persist with it, or by the die-hard gewürztraminer supporters in New Zealand, or in Alsace from where it originally came) gewürztraminer combines all that intense, exotic fruit with a complex spicy dryness, making it a great wine to have with food.

The Seafood Whites

A blistering hot day by the pool. On the table in front of you is a huge platter of grilled seafood piled high, all pink shells and tentacles and succulent flesh and plump bivalves. What are you going to drink? An old red wine? Nah. A big oaky chardonnay? Uh-uh. Lots of cold, fruity, uncomplicated, refreshing, unwooded white wine? Yes, please.

CHENIN BLANC
A grape originally found in the Loire Valley in France — a place where they serve pretty good seafood — and transported to the New World, particularly South Africa and Australia. It's often used to bulk up a blend with other white grapes because of its fairly neutral-tasting, simple fruitiness. But on its own, and when it's

good, chenin blanc can make a very attractive, dry, unwooded, green apple-flavoured wine. In the Loire, and sometimes in South Africa, it produces some stunningly rich, long-lived sweet wines, but few producers elsewhere in the world have really explored chenin blanc in this way.

PINOT GRIS

Also known as pinot grigio (*grigio* is Italian, and *gris* is French for grey), this white grape (well, more of a grey-pink grape like gewürztraminer, but makes a water-white wine) is a newcomer to the New World, but looks set for a healthy future. In Italy, pinot grigio produces crisp whites with melon, nuts and honey flavours: perfect seafood wines. In Alsace, pinot gris, it makes fuller-bodied, dry, spicy white wines, perfect with the onion tarts and charcuterie of the region. In Australia and New Zealand you could expect something between the two styles. Still a very new variety in the New World, but watch out for it.

VERDELHO

Verdelho is grown with conviction in only two places in the world: on the small Atlantic island of Madeira, where it produces a medium-dry fortified wine; and in Australia, where it is usually made into a dry, or off-dry white wine. Very flowery, citrussy and appealing, verdelho can have some of the grassiness of sauvignon blanc and the lemony flavour of semillon when it's good, and also has the potential to age well — if it weren't so damned delicious when it was young. Some Australian wineries put their verdelho in oak barrels and I wish they wouldn't: the wine just ends up smelling of oak, and all that citrussy verdelho character gets lost.

COLOMBARD

Ah, colombard. Poor old colombard. Shunned by 'serious' winemakers but lapped up by everyday drinkers, colombard could probably take the award as the ultimate seafood white wine. It's never going to make anything breathtakingly good, but can be relied upon to produce an endless supply of gluggable, fruity, crisp white wine (and isn't that what we're after here?), often blended with other grapes like chenin blanc. When it's ripe, colombard can have really pungent tropical fruit flavours but manages to hang on to enough acidity to balance the exuberance.

The Honeysuckle Whites

These three grape varieties are planted in such small quantities (in comparison to the endless fields of chardonnay) that they don't strictly deserve more than a passing mention. But they are so well suited to the Australian climate, and produce wines that are so delicious with the ever-popular Mediterranean diet, that I've given them a whole spread to themselves. Who knows? Perhaps we'll be seeing a lot more of them in the future, and forewarned is forearmed.

They're often lumped together as the Rhône whites because, like the red grapes shiraz, grenache and mourvèdre, they originally came from vineyards in France's Rhône Valley. There they are often blended with each other, and are sometimes even chucked in with the black syrah grapes — as shiraz is known in France — to give a bit of lift and perfume to the resulting red wine.

MARSANNE AND ROUSSANNE

A mass of contradictions, is marsanne. There it is in the glass, water-white, flashes of emerald-green light sparkling in the sun. It looks like a bone dry wine. Stick your nose in the glass and up comes this smell like a garden full of flowers, with baskets of ripe nectarines strategically placed under the honeysuckle bush in the shade. Right, so this must be a sweet wine then. Take a sip and there's that perfumed, aromatic

Brown muscat's hedonistic flavours and slippery sweetness could convince the most rabid atheist of the existence of some kind of higher being.

fruitiness, but bugger me if the wine isn't crisp, refreshing and definitely, deliciously dry. Marsanne is like this when it's young, but, like semillon and riesling, if it's made without any ageing in barrel it can also develop very well with a decade or so in bottle into a full, golden and complex drink.

Roussanne is marsanne's big brother. Not as delicately and sweetly perfumed as marsanne, roussanne has more of a feral edge to it: some ripe stone fruit characters, some citrussy smells, but lots of hay and herbal flavours, too. Most often used in blends, and seldom encountered on its own.

VIOGNIER

In the northern Rhône Valley, viognier can produce the most hedonistic white wines that reek of ripe apricots, and grilled nuts and spice, and loads of other goodies that are hugely powerful in the mouth, are rich and sometimes seductive and oily. So you can see why people in other parts of the world are keen to try to emulate this style. Trouble is that viognier is the most difficult of these three varieties to grow well; but then this only adds to the challenge for winemakers. Early signs from cooler areas in Australia and other places such as California are promising. Watch out for this one, too. It may be a flash in the pan, but it may be something exciting.

Others

THE MUSCATS

There are two types of muscat grapes — brown muscat and muscat gordo blanco — and it's important not to confuse them. Brown muscat (or frontignac, or *muscat blanc à petits grains* in

French) is so called because the grape is as likely to be dark coloured as light. It can make a pleasant dry white wine with a floral, musky, very grapey smell, but when it's made into a sweet wine it can drive you bonkers with its lusciousness. Either as a fresh, tangerine- and orange-peel-flavoured sweet wine from the Mediterranean, or in an impossibly intense fortified form as one of the great gifts of nature, Australian liqueur muscat, this grape's hedonistic flavours and slippery sweetness could convince the most rabid atheist of the existence of some kind of higher being. Muscat gordo blanco, on the other hand (or lexia, or muscat of Alexandria, or straight gordo), is nowhere near as revered, and is either made into fairly unexciting sweet white wine or sold as dried grapes.

MUSCADELLE

You'd be really hard-pressed to find a bottle of wine with the name 'muscadelle' on it. In Bordeaux it is sometimes part of the blend with semillon and sauvignon blanc in the white wines of the region (both dry and sweet), and that's about it until you get to Australia — north-eastern Victoria in particular — where it is the grape responsible for the fortified sweet wines called 'tokay'. These wines are, at their best, luscious, treacly wines with a not-unpleasant smell of stewed tea and toffee, and with not quite as much of the exuberant fruitiness you'd find in muscats from the same place.

UGNI BLANC OR TREBBIANO

Now a grape with a dreary name like ugni blanc is kind of telling you before you even think about pulling the cork not to expect much, isn't it? But then, when was the last time you found ugni blanc, or its pseudonym trebbiano, on a wine label? Not too recently, I'll bet. Because although there are an awful lot of ugni blanc vines in the ground all over the world, it seldom makes it to top billing. Why? Because it makes a clean, dry white wine with a startling lack of flavour — perfect for blending with other things, or distilling into brandy. And that's usually what happens to it.

PALOMINO AND PEDRO XIMINEZ

Very important grapes in Spain, producing a style of wine sadly declining in popularity: sherry. Palomino has just the right low acid and neutral flavour required for dry styles of sherry like fino and manzanilla, and pedro has the ability to get really ripe — important for sweeter styles of sherry. There's still quite a bit of palomino planted in Australia and South Africa — a hangover from the days when both countries produced a lot of fortified wine.

SULTANA, DORADILLO, WALTHAM CROSS

Look familiar? Yes, it's true, the humble sultana and waltham cross grapes that you pick up from your local fruit shop could, but for a cruel twist of fate, have ended up as wine in that four-litre cask in your fridge. These are affectionately known as the multi-purpose grapes, and they share one common link: they are probably more fun to eat than drink. But without them we wouldn't have a cask wine market, we wouldn't have dirt cheap bubbly and we wouldn't have some really quite wonderful Australian brandies. So don't knock 'em; these grape varieties have come in quite handy over the years.

Red

About
red grapes

Pinot Noir

You know those old Tex Avery cartoons where the sleazy dog is sitting at a table in a Wild West town and the impossibly curvaceous singer comes on and the dog's eyes pop out across the room and his jaw thumps to the floor and steam comes out of his ears? Wine made from pinot noir can have a similar effect.

Now before you go rushing off to buy a truck load, read that again very carefully. Pinot noir can do that to you, but it does so only very rarely. Pinot noir can also be the grape responsible for some of the most *un*memorable bottles of plonk you'll ever come across.

Pinot noir is one of the most infuriating red grape varieties. It can be difficult to grow and prefers cooler climates, where it can take most advantage of the long, slow ripening period to develop lots of complex flavours. That's why it usually does best in chilly areas like Burgundy in France, New Zealand's South Island, Oregon in the US and Tasmania. (You'll also find pinot noir in the cooler spots when it's being grown for sparkling wine use. Pinot noir juice is much prized by bubbly makers because of the full flavour it can give to a blend.)

Pinot noir is very fussy about the climate it's grown in, and tends to make terribly dilute wines if cropped too many tonnes to the hectare. Wines made from this variety generally have a less opaque red colour, softer tannins and more delicate aromas than those made from other varieties.

At its most basic, pinot should have flavours like red berries, strawberry and cherry. A little further up the quality scale, you might find spices such as clove and aniseed, and perhaps a good whack of earthiness, gaminess or undergrowth-like pungency. When it's good, pinot noir also has a softness, a velvety texture in the mouth, and, when it's really, really, write-home-about good, an ethereal, elusive, totally seductive perfume which can become stunningly complex with five to ten years in the bottle.

So if at first you don't succeed with pinot noir, and keep coming across the less impressive bottles, persevere. One day, you'll pour yourself a glass of innocent-looking, pale brick-red liquid, stick your nose in and take a deep sniff, and your eyes will pop out, your jaw will drop to the floor and steam will come out of your ears. Well I hope so, anyway.

The Cabernet Family

CABERNET SAUVIGNON

If chardonnay is the Coke of the wine world, what does that make cabernet? The Pepsi?

Like chardonnay, cabernet sauvignon is grown everywhere, ripens fairly reliably (although late in the season, making it not too common in really cool areas), is relatively easy to make into good wine, and has easily understandable, very attractive flavours. From Bordeaux to Bulgaria, from Coonawarra to Cape Town, from the Napa Valley to New Zealand, sturdy cabernet sauvignon vines are churning out deeply coloured red wine that smells of blackcurrants, is firm and tannic, and can age well.

As long as it gets enough sun to ripen it, cabernet sauvignon is a grape growers' dream, with long bunches of small, thick-skinned fruit that is fairly resistant to disease. Those thick skins give cabernet sauvignon wine its *oomph*: lots of colour, lots of potentially complex flavours, and generous tannin — that astringent substance that makes your gums pucker up and helps a red wine age well in bottle.

Cabernet sauvignon has a reputation for producing very long-lived wines. The grape is a major component of the great clarets of Bordeaux, wines which, when they're really good, can taste utterly delicious and almost incomparably complex for twenty, fifty, even a hundred years. That's why it's planted all over the world: if you want to make a wine that is almost guaranteed to improve with age, even outlive you, then cabernet sauvignon is the grape variety to use.

But that's not all it's good for. Most of the cabernet sauvignon in the world goes to make much simpler, though still delicious, medium-to full-bodied red wine that is drunk very young. And to help soften cabernet sauvignon's naturally high tannin, the grape is often blended with other varieties, usually within what has come to be known affectionately as the cabernet family.

CABERNET FRANC

If grapes had emotions, cabernet franc would be eternally frustrated. Although it shares the same first name as its illustrious cousin cabernet sauvignon, cabernet franc just doesn't manage to cut the mustard in quite the same way.

It is similar in appearance on the vine, and makes a fragrant, blackcurrant-smelling wine, but (with a few notable exceptions) it doesn't have the body, the tannin structure or the complexity of the other grape. This doesn't stop quite a few producers in places such as the Loire Valley and Australia releasing very drinkable, leafy, attractive straight cabernet franc wines.

Ah, but blend a little of this spritely, perfumed stuff with some chunky, dense cabernet sauvignon and watch in wonderment as the two merge into a whole that is greater than the sum of its parts. And why stop there? In Bordeaux, and increasingly in other parts of the world, winemakers have discovered that these aren't the only two grapes that blend well together.

MERLOT

If only all red grapes could make wines that were so downright cuddly as merlot. Not that merlot can't produce big, serious, stern wines that benefit from spending decades in a cool, dark place. It can and does in places like St Emilion and Pomerol near Bordeaux, the regions that made merlot's name. But there's an inherent suppleness and roundness to merlot that, try as you might, you can't really avoid.

That's why this lovely red grape is used so much in blends with cabernet sauvignon. It's not as tannic as cabernet, and hasn't as much acid, so it fills out the middle of cabernet's astringency and not only helps the blend taste more complete but also helps the wine drink better earlier.

But merlot has a good future in Australia and other parts of the New World on its own, as a varietal wine. The same assets it has as a blender — easy early drinking, finer, softer tannins and sheer suppleness — can combine with a fragrance of berries, damson plums and fruitcake to make very gluggable red wine. But, as some growers are finding out, merlot can be more temperamental in the vineyard than sturdy old cabernet, responding strongly to

If only all red grapes could make wines that were so downright cuddly as merlot.

where it's planted: the vine doesn't like unstable weather during the crucial flowering stage, for example. Bottle shop shelves may soon start to groan with merlot, there's so much being planted, and among them we should be able to find more than the occasional very good drink.

MALBEC AND PETIT VERDOT

These two grapes complete the big, happy cabernet family. Both usually appear only in minor supporting roles in blends with the other grapes, added for their deep colour and slightly coarse, rustic character. It is extremely unusual to find petit verdot as a wine in its own right, as few people have explored its charms, but malbec has done quite well for itself as a varietal wine. In south-west France, Argentina and the warmer areas of Australia it is capable of making juicy, dark, brambly red wines.

The Spice of Life

SHIRAZ

Shiraz. Just roll that word around in your mouth for a while. Lovely, isn't it?

Play with it on your tongue and it can conjure up images of spice bazaars and hermits on steep, rocky hills and damp, red Australian soil (it helps here to have had a few glasses first). Shiraz. So comforting. One of the nicest words in the world of wine.

Shiraz is a grape with a history. The rather romantic story goes that the vine was first cultivated in a serious way thousands of years ago near the Persian city of — you guessed it — Shiraz, then taken by either the Romans or the Phoenicians out into the Mediterranean and up the Rhône river into France. (Obviously this didn't just happen one balmy afternoon in summer; it took a few generations.)

The shiraz vine loved being in the Rhône Valley: the climate was hot and the steep hilly soils were rocky and mean — perfect for growing good grapes. It didn't take long for shiraz (syrah) to start forging a name for itself as the grape responsible for some of France's richest, darkest, most seductive red wines — called Hermitage and Côte-Rôtie. Luckily, the Rhône was one of the places that early Australian wine pioneers like James Busby visited in the early nineteenth century, looking for grape vines to transport to the new colony. And even more luckily, syrah/shiraz was one of the vines they chose.

As soon as it arrived, shiraz (often under the pseudonym hermitage, after its homeland) ran amok, covering the new, hot, red country with its vines. It loved being here almost as much as being in the Old World and it is still the most widely planted red grape variety in Australia.

Originally this grape was popular because it just did an honest day's work and didn't complain. Shiraz will grow in almost any climate, from hot to cool, and can be used to make all kinds of wine styles, from light reds, through big reds and sparkling reds, into port styles. And that's how it was used traditionally: as a workhorse, not particularly respected as a premium grape.

Today, things are different. Shiraz is enjoying a reversal of fortune, viewed as Australia's quintessential red variety, with grapes squeezed out by low-yielding, warm-grown, century-old shiraz vines prized as some of the most valuable in the country. These grapes make the 'traditional' style of shiraz: inky black in colour, full of rich, ripe blackberry fruit and often accompanied by slabs of vanilla oak flavour from time spent in barrel. But there's another style emerging, one made from grapes grown in cooler climates such as that of southern Victoria. This style of shiraz is a lighter-bodied red wine, with more raspberry-like fruit and spicy, peppery smells.

The other great thing about shiraz, apart from its adaptability, is its suitability as a blending grape. Shiraz wine usually has a big round generosity of flavour right on the middle of the tongue, and this can come in handy in a blend with cabernet, which is notorious for being a bit hollow-tasting when it's young. Shiraz/cabernet blends aren't as common as they were, which is a shame, because the two grapes work well together. It's far trendier to blend your shiraz with other grapes that also originally came from the Rhône Valley, like grenache or mourvèdre.

GRENACHE

Talk about a renaissance. If you'd bowled up to an Australian winemaker ten years ago and told him or her that grenache was going to be one of *the* red varieties of the 1990s, he or she would have laughed in your face. Not a polite little laugh, either. A big, rude, hurtful, don't-be-so-bloody-stupid laugh. The joke would be on them though, because grenache is indeed thoroughly modish at present.

There's always been a lot of grenache planted in Australia, just as there's a lot of it planted in other warm-climate regions around the world, like Spain and the south of France — and for the same reason: it can reliably produce large crops of very ripe grapes. The trouble is, the larger the crop, the lower the quality. Until recently in Australia, grenache was being cropped heavily and used for cheap bulk wine, fortified wine and rosé, with the grape's name hardly ever appearing on the label.

Then shiraz got all popular again and

winemakers began taking another look at their other vineyards full of old vines. They realised that, if you don't crop the grenache too high, it is possible to make a seriously good red out of it. And suddenly that's what everyone was doing. But apart from the very best examples, grenache always seems to lack something as a red wine varietal. Vibrant colour, bags of spice, ripe, scrumptious fruit and never wanting for alcohol, but just not totally satisfying on the palate. And so that's where these other spicy grapes come in — as components of a blend.

Mataro or mourvèdre

Along with a renewed interest in grenache came the resurrection of mataro. Mataro used to be grown quite widely in warm areas in Australia (and like grenache is still common in places such as southern France and Spain). But, again, it was just too easy to make into an ordinary wine, and had declined in popularity. Then the new winemakers 'rediscovered' their old, low-yielding mataro vines, rechristened them with the trendy French name of mourvèdre and — hey presto — came up with another hip, hyped variety. Mourvèdre (or mataro) works best when it's in a blend with shiraz or grenache. On its own it tends to taste a little hard and earthy.

The Italian Mob

The Italian grape varieties could be the great red hope for interesting drinking. Originally responsible for some of Italy's greatest wines, they have been transported to the New World by pioneering producers looking for new flavours — different flavours, flavours that don't have anything in common with the dominant grapes like cabernet. It's early days yet, but there could be serious room for these grapes in Australian bottles in the future.

Nebbiolo

Of all Italian grapes, nebbiolo is the one that might take the most getting used to. It comes from Piemonte, in Italy's north-west, and is a grape renowned for making red wines with huge, aggressive, furry tannins. But despite that, the romantic nebbiolo (it's named after the *nebbia*, or fogs that fill the steep-sided valleys of the region) can also have the most alluring smells and flavours — roses, bitumen, undergrowth and roasting meat, for example. My mouth is watering already, and that's the point: nebbiolo wines, and wines made from these other Italian grape varieties are often much better when drunk with food than on their own. They are less obviously fruity than varieties like cabernet, and have firmer tannins to match full-flavoured food.

Dolcetto

Dolcetto is also from Piemonte, but it is about as far from nebbiolo as you can get. Unlike nebbiolo, dolcetto seldom has much tannin to get in the way of easy understanding, and this means it doesn't age as well in the bottle (nebbiolo can age well for years). Dolcetto is all about drinking now: it makes wines that are bright purple, light- to medium-bodied and crammed with juicy, spicy berry fruit. They just cry out to be quaffed almost as soon as they've been bottled.

BARBERA

Barbera is another Piemontese grape, and it lies somewhere between the first two. It makes wines that are fuller than dolcetto but not as tannic as nebbiolo, have firmer berry fruit than dolcetto but not as much complexity as nebbiolo, can be drunk younger than nebbiolo but last longer than dolcetto.

SANGIOVESE

Although sangiovese is the grape mainly responsible for the sea of cheap chianti drunk in Italian restaurants the world over, there is much more to this noble Tuscan variety than that. After all, if your name translated as 'the blood of Jupiter', you'd want to make your mark on the world other than in countless raffia-covered bottles. When it's good, as the top Italian producers in places like Tuscany and Emilia Romagna have shown, sangiovese is capable of producing wonderful briary, earthy, complex red wines, with dark cherry fruit, tight tannins and a capacity to age well. It has also been planted in California and increasingly in Australia, with encouraging results.

The Others

DURIF

Durif could easily be lumped in with the Italian mob because although it originally comes from the south of France, in warm places like Rutherglen in Australia it can produce very Italian-tasting red wine: earthy, dark and delicious.

ZINFANDEL

This variety is planted mainly in California, where it's the American answer to shiraz — there's lots of it, it goes into everything from rosé to port, it's full of fruit and spice, and it can reach high alcohol levels. In Australia, small pockets are planted, most notably in Margaret River, where it makes a solid, alcoholic purple wine that needs hearty foods to match it.

GAMAY

What does the word *beaujolais* conjure up for you? Probably images of bright-crimson, lolly-flavoured, light red wine, possibly chilled, and drunk in summer. That's fine, except good beaujolais, from Beaujolais, south of Burgundy in France, is a much more satisfying drink altogether, and it's made from gamay grapes. Certainly, gamay will never make a big, rich wine, and should always have a certain delicacy, but the image of most Australian 'beaujolais' has done the variety no justice. Gamay is like a slightly less complex version of pinot noir, often with more up-front strawberry, cherry, raspberry fruit when it is young and not quite the same capacity to age, but often with spicy, earthy characters nonetheless.

TOURIGA

One of the major grape varieties in the port-producing Douro Valley in Portugal. Australian winemakers who want to make serious vintage port that can age for decades will think very long and hard about finding some touriga vines. The grapes have just the right type of tannins, dense, raisiny fruit flavours and the capacity to get very ripe — all the things you need for good port. Apart from Portugal, there are only small plantings in Australia and elsewhere, probably because few people are seriously interested in producing port these days.

PINOT MEUNIER

Pinot meunier is only very occasionally made into a red wine, even though, as the name suggests, it is similar to pinot noir. It is far more common to find a pinot meunier component in sparkling wine — and then it is only the juice, taken off the grape skins before any colour can be leeched from them — where it is blended with chardonnay and, funnily enough, pinot noir. Pinot meunier is useful in a sparkling wine blend because it is low in acid and develops quickly, giving early drinkability and a honeyed richness.

TEMPRANILLO

Hardly ever seen outside its native Spain, which is a surprise, because tempranillo can make quite delicious red wine. When it's really good, as in the best wines of the Ribera del Duero region, tempranillo combines the intense berry fruit of cabernet with the generosity of shiraz and the earthiness of sangiovese. Just waiting to be leapt upon as the Next Big Thing.

CINSAUT AND CARIGNAN

Even though they're not at all widely planted in Australia these two standby red grapes get a mention, just for completeness' sake. In southern France they're common, often blended with other spicy grapes, such as grenache, to make the bottomless lake of red wine consumed with hearty Mediterranean and Provençal cooking.

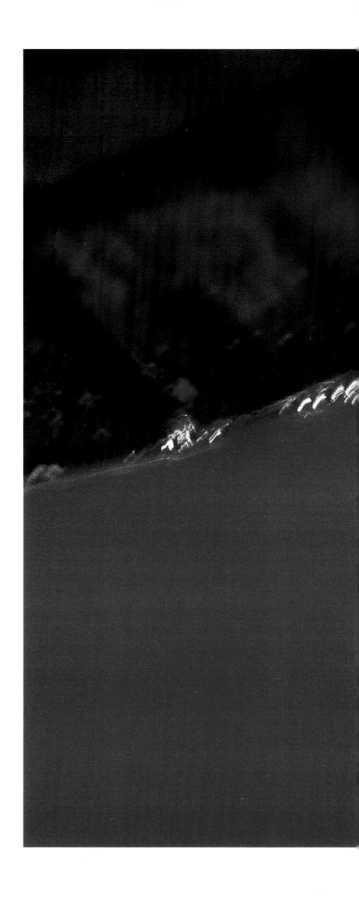

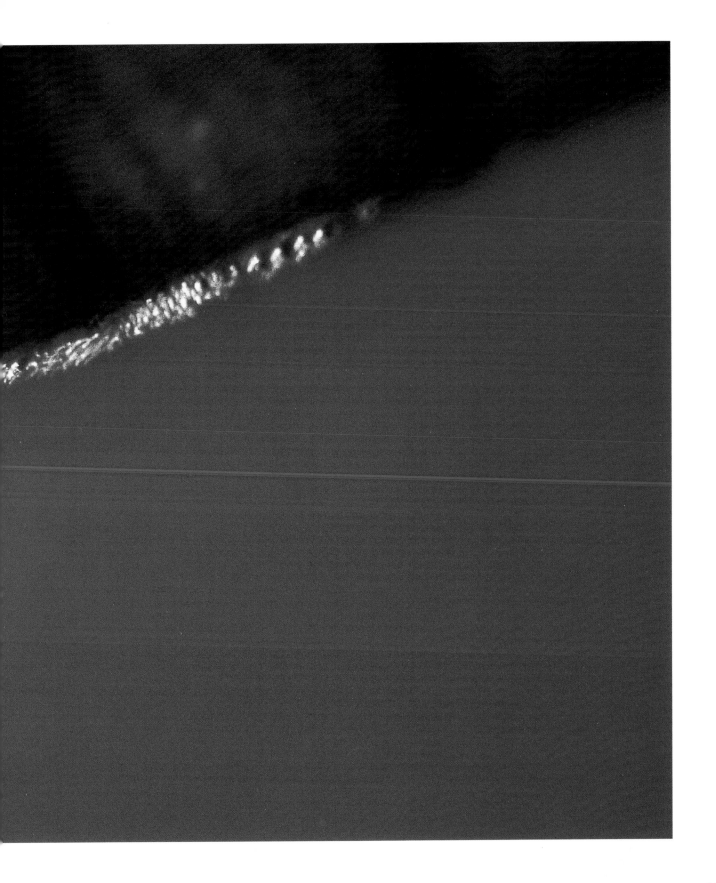

Air
About climate

Vineyards all look pretty much the same from the air. As our tiny plane makes its descent into the sun-parched Upper Hunter Valley in New South Wales, we pass over square patches of alternating green and ochre lines, neat rows contrasting with the surrounding wild, dusty, olive-coloured forests.

The plane buzzes a couple of wineries, then comes down fast, landing on a makeshift airstrip. We get out and it's stiflingly hot, even without the plane's blasting exhaust. It's still the height of summer for most of Australia, but here they're moving into autumn and have started the harvest already.

After the grape variety used, a vineyard's location has the most impact on how the resulting wine will taste — especially on that wine's eventual style. Hot climates tend to produce bigger, riper-tasting wines than do cool climates. Here in the Upper Hunter, they get quite a bit of sun and lots of heat. Because of that, grapes ripen quickly, producing heaps of flavour and sugar, but sometimes losing the all-important balancing acid at the same time.

They get little rainfall during the summer in this warm climate, and sometimes not much during winter either. The rain mostly falls just when they don't need it — at harvest time — but this year it's holding off for now. Warm climates can be quite difficult to grow really good grapes in, but the Upper Hunter growers manage quite well.

We've come to taste some chardonnay grapes. There's lots of chardonnay planted here, and because of the warmth of the climate, it usually makes a rich, ripe-tasting white wine. The grapes that we taste, plucked from the vine, are sweet, soft, honeyed, quite luscious.

Leap forward in time. It's almost two months later and we're back in the plane, heading south, to Tasmania. As white-crested blue waves give way to the island's coastline, lush green forests sweep under the wings. We land in the Pipers Brook region, its gentle hills rolling away from the wide Tamar River. As we get out, a chilly breeze whips past us, rushing up into the surrounding vineyards, tearing at the leaves, making tight bunches of chardonnay shudder.

The grapes are being picked, even though they are nowhere near as ripe as the chardonnay in the Hunter was. In fact, biting into some berries is quite a shock: they taste almost tart, very lemony, with lots of acid tingling on the tongue. These grapes will be made into sparkling wine and they're perfect for that: you want lots of acidity and those fine, citric flavours to make your bubbly crisp and refreshing.

Even if they were left on the vine for longer to achieve the same sugar levels as the grapes in the Hunter they wouldn't have the same flavours or make the same style of wine. The climate is cooler here in northern Tasmania and the ripening season is longer, meaning the grapes ripen more slowly, retaining more acid and developing subtler flavours.

Back in the plane once more and over to Margaret River, in Western Australia. There's plenty of chardonnay here, too, and while it's not as hot as the Hunter here, it's not as cool as Tasmania either, so while that crucial ripening period can be wonderfully slow, the grapes do actually ripen fully without much trouble.

We stop at a vineyard and munch on some chardonnay berries. They are ripe — not as rich and luscious as the Hunter grapes, but sweet nonetheless. Not as tart and citrussy as the Tasmanian grapes, but definitely with good crisp acid. And the wines? Places that balance enough heat with enough cold and enough sun with enough rain (in most years), like Margaret River, are regarded as the best places to grow grapes. The proof of it all is in the eating — and the drinking.

Earth
About soil

I'm on my hands and knees in the middle of a vineyard by the side of the highway in Coonawarra, South Australia. I'm burrowing around under some old cabernet sauvignon vines, my nose almost touching the dirt. And what dirt! It's the colour of Uluru at sunset, a glowing, luminescent red that shines blindingly up at me in the sun. It smells like pure, good soil should smell: slightly sweet, delicious, almost edible.

I dig down only a few centimetres with my hands and begin to see chunks of ivory-white limestone. If I keep digging, I'll hit a solid block of this chalky stuff.

I get up, dust myself off and walk twenty metres up a dirt road that runs away from the highway. Here the soil isn't that glowing red any more. It's a black–brown, kind-of dull-looking clay that runs deeper than the red stuff. There are some old cabernet vines here, too, and the fruit from both vineyards is made by the same winemaker.

The funny thing is that, although the two vineyards are almost identical — same grape variety, same climate, same rainfall, same amount of sunshine, and so on — the wines taste different. And not only that, but the wine made from grapes grown on the *red* soil is consistently better.

You see, that thick layer of limestone under the red dirt lies over a water table: a soil profile that is about as close to perfection as any cabernet grower could wish for. The surrounding black dirt just isn't as good for grapes.

Traditional, hard-nosed, technologically minded Australian winemakers will admit that the soil you plant your vine in affects the flavour and quality of the resulting wine. They will also admit that some grape varieties do better in certain types of soil. But that's as far as they usually go; they tell you that it's all just a matter of common sense.

The slightly more romantic French (and more open-minded New World winemakers) will put such differences down to *terroir*, a word that links the soil in with all the other physical factors that make up a vine's environment (the slope of the hill, the rainfall, the climate, to name a few), then mixes in a dash of mystery — suggesting there is perhaps some literal flavour exchange between the vineyard and the wine it produces.

Now I'm standing in a cold vineyard in Chablis, in northern France. The chardonnay grapes on the vines here look just like chardonnay grapes on vines in the Adelaide Hills, in California's Napa Valley, just the same as grapes on the vines grown a few kilometres down the road in Burgundy. But the dry white wine made here in Chablis tastes different from the dry white wine made in all those other places. When it's good, it has this unmistakable flinty character, a mineral-like flavour that can be akin to sucking on river pebbles (honestly).

I look down at the soil and see that it's littered with big grey shards of pale, flinty quartz. And the better vineyards here, the ones that give more of that unmistakable Chablis character in their wines, have more flinty stuff in the soil. Coincidence? *Mais non, monsieur. Ça c'est terroir.*

Soil for growing vines has to have three ideal environments: good drainage, to encourage the vines to send their roots burrowing down into the rock; the right chemical composition; and an ability to store and re-radiate the sun's heat. After that, anything else is a bonus. And whether you agree with the hard-nosed view of science or the romantic view of *terroir* is entirely up to you; it's an argument that's been going for a long time, and looks set to go on for a few years yet.

Water

About vines

In the dry cool of a late summer dusk, the Barossa Valley takes on an enchanted air. As I walk back from the pub past an ancient vineyard of shiraz, the fluid purple light plays tricks with my eyes: the stubby old vines look for all the world like they're trying to claw their way out of the stony soil. Thick stumps of wood, they are weathered, twisted, arthritic, their spindly black arms punctuated by tufts of foliage, half disguising clusters of dark-blue grapes.

These vines have been producing fruit since the turn of the century. While war twice raged in Europe they soaked up the warm Barossa sun and converted the energy to sugar. As presidents and prime ministers came and went, these vines sucked water from deep below the Barossa soil and bled it out again in the form of juice. Before my grandfather was born, these vines were making wine.

Because they are so old, these vines yield only a tiny crop of grapes. And because the yield is so low, the flavours and sugars in the fruit are super-concentrated, resulting in an equally powerful, concentrated wine.

When these vines were planted, it was common practice to let the plants grow like a small bush, or to train them up to a single low wire. Fruit was low to the ground, picking it was back-breaking, and the vines grew in this gnarly, buckled way over the decades. When this vineyard was planted, there was no irrigation installed. The vines had to probe

deep into the ground searching for enough water to survive and to ripen their grapes. In dry years, the vines suffered from lack of water and the already small yield shrank even more.

But this vineyard is not typical in Australia. Next to it in the gathering dark is a much more usual example: tall, flourishing, overflowing with tendrils and canes and foliage. The vines were planted ten years ago, and from the beginning have been watered via the black pipes that run under each row. They have been carefully trained up on a complex system of wires that lifts the lush green canopy above head height, exposing a large crop of grapes, shining in the gloom.

These vines are just approaching their first flush of maturity. Because of the supplementary watering and the modern growing methods, they produce five times as much fruit as the venerable old vines next door, and the way the vines are trained enables the fruit to be harvested by machine — all of which leads to more economically viable wine production.

This vineyard *could*, with overwatering and a particular kind of vine trellising, produce over twelve tonnes of grapes per hectare, but the resulting wine would taste dilute and would lack the concentration that good shiraz should have. But the wine made from these vines *is* good shiraz, because the grower keeps the yield to about seven tonnes per hectare.

There are almost as many ways of growing vines as there are vineyards in the world. Different ways of training the vines, different planting density per hectare, different approaches to irrigation — or the lack of it. But every grower who is committed to quality is searching for the same thing: balance. That's the key. A balanced vineyard should produce good grapes and good wine — as long as the season is kind.

Sun

About seasons

The rain's coming down so fast, I can't make out whether the old man's face is wet from the weather or wet from tears. The heavy clouds above us have darkened everything, and a battered Akubra shadows his face even more.

We're walking through the old man's vineyard, mud caking our boots so efficiently that it feels like walking through a swimming pool. The rain makes such a racket as it hurtles down on the overflowing vine leaves that I can't make out what the old man's saying. Perhaps he's just muttering to himself. Occasionally he stops and pulls off a bunch of grapes from under the leafy canopy, inspects them and drops them into the mud, not so much in disgust as in resignation.

The grapes look ripe to me, but the old man shouts through the rain that they needed another week of sunshine before they could be picked and all he got was this bloody storm and it's the first real bloody rain they've had all season it would have to come now of all times and who in their right mind would be a bloody grape grower anyway, all the stress it causes and if it carries on it's going to turn out to be a bloody terrible vintage.

To a wine drinker, *vintage* is the most beautiful word in the English language. Vintage sums up all that is most exciting about wine — the fact that, each year, a new grape harvest throughout the globe produces millions of bottles of wine that are different in some way from the millions of bottles that have gone before. Since each wine is guaranteed to taste at least slightly different every year because of what happens during vintage, it's just impossible to get bored by it all.

To a winemaker, each vintage is exciting because it offers a new opportunity to make the best wine possible, to try out new techniques and learn from previous vintages (they get only one crack at it every twelve months, after all). But the fact that no vintage is quite like any other can also be a problem.

The quality of a vintage — signified by the year stated on the label — depends not just on what the weather was like when the grapes were picked. It also derives from what happened during the seasons leading up to the harvest. An ideal set of events might run something like this.

Winter. The vines are naked, scrawny in the cold. They have been pruned back over the last couple of months, the pruners carefully leaving a certain number of buds on each cane. The vines lie dormant, resistant to frosts.

Spring. Those buds begin to burst as the weather warms: small, downy green flashes bright against the dark wood. Over the next few weeks the buds turn into shoots, which turn into new young canes with bright-green leaves. The weather is warming, dry, with occasional rain to keep the vine flourishing.

Early summer. The green shoots produce tiny flowers which, in the gentle breeze, fertilise and set small clusters of what will become fruit. The weather is still warm, with the odd shower.

Summer. Over the next few months, the tiny clusters swell out into small, hard, green grapes. As the perfect summer weather continues (warm days, cool nights, only very occasional showers to keep the vine healthy) the grapes ripen, changing colour. This is called 'veraison' — it is when the red grapes darken and the white grapes become translucent.

Early autumn. The warm weather miraculously continues right through picking, and the grapes are all harvested at perfect ripeness. After the picking is over, the rains come, replenishing the soil and the dams. The celebrations begin.

Winter. The vines go to sleep. Pruning starts again. Everybody's happy.

Now I don't have to tell you that the above is a fantasy. Nature is hardly ever so kind. Sometimes a vineyard, a wine region, even a whole country or the world, experiences a season something like perfection (a good example is 1990, which seems to have been a great vintage worldwide) and it's immediately hailed as a classic year or the 'vintage of the century'.

Reality, of course, is much more down to earth. Late frosts can viciously burn off those tender young buds in spring, destroying the potential crop. The rain can start in early summer and continue until after picking, creating problems with rotten grapes, disease in the vines, and dilute wine. Or the rain can refuse to come for months, and leave the vines struggling, stressed and unable to grow enough foliage to capture enough sun to ripen the grapes. Or the season can be perfect until picking, and then the clouds can open. Or the season can be lousy until picking, when the sun can come out at the last moment and rescue everything.

You just can't win. Who would be a grape grower?

Winter. The vines are naked,
scrawny in the cold. They
have been pruned back over
the last couple of months,
the pruners carefully leaving
a certain number of buds on
each cane.

Harvest
About picking

We get up at 4 am. It isn't even beginning to get light. We gather outside the winery in the dark and the cold. It has been a crystal-clear night, no moon, and all of yesterday's blistering heat has disappeared.

The chill bites into my hangover. We stayed up late last night, lingering over the barbecue, drinking too many older vintages of the winery's premium cabernet. But there is no time to worry about that now. We are each given our snippers and told to follow the tractor out to one of the shiraz blocks halfway up the hill.

Further up the hill, a machine harvester stands out against the greying morning sky like something out of *Close Encounters*, lights and noise grinding into the still air as it finishes straddling the last row of chardonnay. The beaters on the big machine have now spent almost two hours thrashing at the vines, shaking the grapes from their stalks.

The fruit has been trucked swiftly down to the winery, to be crushed and pressed while it is still cool, so that the flavour is retained in the juice and fermentation can start slowly and gently.

The chardonnay can be picked all at once by machine because it is healthy, but the shiraz vines have some rot running through them, which is why we're going in to pick by hand — to select the good grapes and leave the bad. The shiraz isn't quite as ripe as the winemaker would have liked, but he's made the decision to take it off now, before the rot really takes hold.

We each grab a bucket and trudge down a row, snippers in hand. There is just enough light in the sky now to see which are the good bunches: plump blue berries, full of sugar-rich juice; and which are the bad: shrivelled and dusty with mould. When our buckets are full, they are taken from us and tipped into the big bin on the tractor's trailer.

We carry on like this for hours, bending and snipping, often nicking ourselves, sticky grape juice drying crusty on our hands, until the sun is directly above us. The machine harvester would have taken a couple of hours to do this; we'll take half a day. But machines can't sort the good from the bad, and tend to bruise the grapes. Picking by hand is still the best, if the hardest, way.

It is hot again now as we sit in the vineyard and have lunch. The throbbing in my head has shrunk to a persistent ache. The shiraz grapes have gone down the hill to the winery, to be tipped into a crusher and pumped from there into a big tank to ferment. We eat sandwiches and drink cool water. Images of European vineyard workers tucking into huge meals and knocking back gallons of rough red wine (and that's just breakfast) flashed through my mind. In the heat of this Australian vintage, that kind of carry-on would make you faint.

The vineyard manager comes up and tells us there will be no more picking today, but there will be another early start tomorrow, taking fruit off the larger shiraz block. A couple of us head down to the winery, to rake out the spent grape stalks from the crusher, and to heave pipes around from tank to tank. This goes on until it is dark again. Then somebody lights the barbie and pulls out a few bottles of red. It is another late night.

Winery

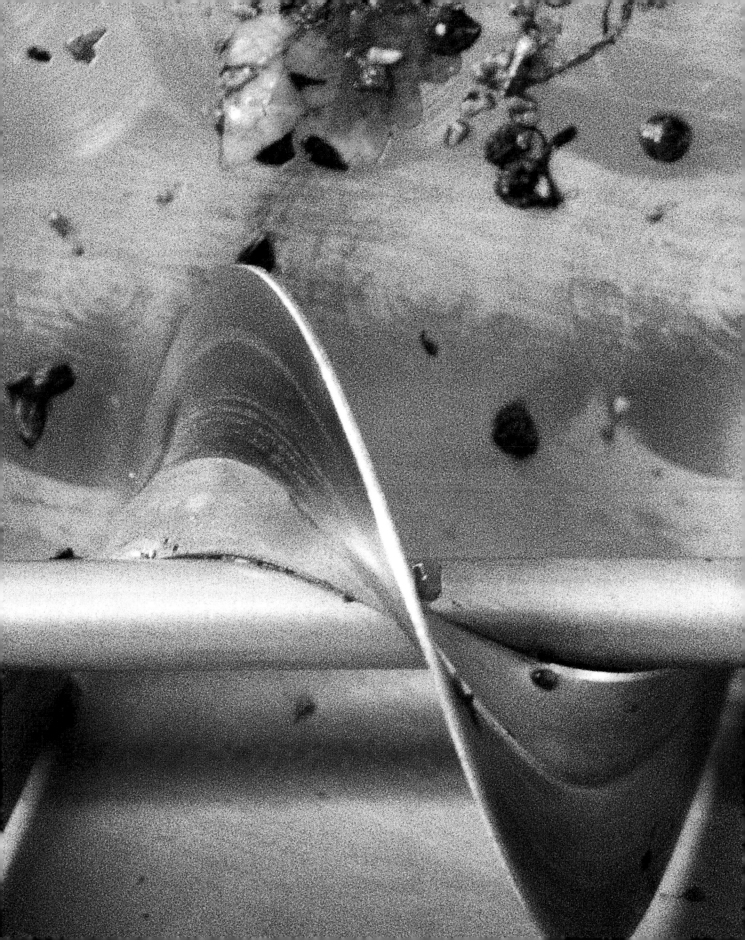

The Styles of Wine

Go to a winery. Put this book down, get a couple of good friends together, get in the car and drive until you get to a winery. I don't care how far you have to drive, and I don't care if you have a job to go to. This is more important.

You'll understand more about winemaking by spending one hour in a winery (preferably but not necessarily at vintage time) than you will by spending a lifetime reading books like this. The big advantage a winery has, apart from giving you the chance to see first hand what's going on, is the smell of the place. Oh, you can *read* about fermentation on the next page and about oak barrels a few pages on from that, but in a winery you can *smell* that mesmerising smell of yeast working away and you can stick your nose inside a barrel and breathe in all its delicious vanilla toast aromas yourself. In a winery, you can *taste* wine being made.

The winery is where a wine's final style is decided. The way the grapes have been grown and when they were picked have a big influence on style, but once the grapes are off the vine, it's really up to the winemaker to guide them, mould them into the finished product. Grape growers will tell you that 'good wine is made in the vineyard'. The people shovelling grapes into crushers at the winery are more likely to say, 'The best winemaker is the one who stuffs up the fruit the least.'

In an ideal world, if the vineyard is in the right spot, and the grape varieties are the right ones for that spot, and the weather has been kind and the vintage went smoothly, all the winemaker has to do is make sure all the equipment is clean and in the right place and the right order, and the wine will virtually make itself.

In the real world, things are usually less than ideal, and the winemaker at vintage time is a very busy person indeed.

Juice
How wine begins

In the beginning was the grape, and the grape was good.

In fact the grape *is* perfect. Wrapped up in each berry is everything necessary for making wine — water, sugar, acid, flavours. It's as though millions of years of evolution and natural selection led up to the creation of something so perfect that all we humans had to do was come along and realise what nature was handing to us on a plate (or should I say stalk?).

Making wine out of such ideal raw materials as grapes is quite ludicrously simple. The basic recipe runs something like this:

Wine

Ingredients:

grapes

Method:

Jump up and down on the grapes so that the juice comes out and wild yeasts on the skins and in the air can ferment the sugar.

Leave the juice until it has stopped bubbling, and the sugar has turned to alcohol.

Drink.

I mean, how easy is that?

Making *good* wine, on the other hand — wine that is free of faults, that is clear and bright, that has character and body and drinkability and deliciousness — is a little more involved. And whether it's white wine, red wine, dessert wine, sparkling wine or fortified wine that you're after, the process always starts with some gentle violence.

The first thing a winemaker will do to freshly harvested grapes is mash 'em up. It must give grape growers a momentary twinge of pain to see their precious, picture-perfect berries, the product of months of backbreaking tender loving care, being flung rudely into a receival bin and forced through a crushing–destemming machine. It must break their hearts for a second or two to see their blemish-free fruit stripped of its stalks, to witness the skins on each grape being ripped open to release the glistening juicy pulp.

But this gorgeous, flowing, sticky, sweet juice has to be released somehow, so the yeast can get at the sugar. Because it's the seething frenzy of fermentation that follows — yeast converting sugar to alcohol, carbon dioxide and heat — that is the heart and soul of the whole process, the crucial turning point between innocent grape juice and worldly wine.

The first thing a winemaker will do to freshly harvested grapes is mash 'em up. It must break grape growers hearts for a second or two to see their blemish-free fruit stripped of its stalks, to witness the skins on each grape being ripped open to release the glistening juicy pulp.

Steel
How white wines are made

This is the modern winery: a gleaming place, a light-filled place, a shining place, a temple of sparkling stainless steel. All those clean lines, those humming machines, those gauges and dials and valves and pipes. Ah, the hygiene, the hygiene.

Cleanliness is next to godliness in the white-winemaker's dictionary — and it's written in bigger, bolder, brighter letters too. Most modern winemakers would agree that the secret to making good wine — especially white wine — is to make it clean and cool — and the cleaner and cooler the better.

The idea is to control the process as much as possible, to minimise the risks of anything unwanted (like too much oxygen or bacteria) getting at the juice before the winemaker does. Keeping everything cool and clean and efficient helps you stay in control. That's why most harvesting and crushing is preferably done early in the day, before the temperature rises;

why a winemaker's best friend is a plentiful supply of water to keep everything spotless; and why most modern wineries are so blindingly stainless.

The object of making good white wine is to get the juice out of the grapes, to ferment that juice, then bottle the resulting wine while retaining as many as possible of the grape's sometimes-delicate smells and flavours. Once you've done that, you can bottle it almost immediately or play around with it a little, perhaps putting it in some oak barrels to pick up fuller, richer characters.

Let's start with the simplest wines — unwooded dry whites — and see how they are made.

Unwooded (lighter) dry white wine

INGREDIENTS
white grapes (riesling is good but you could use semillon,
sauvignon blanc, colombard, chenin blanc or any number
of other white grapes)
yeast

EQUIPMENT
lots of stainless-steel containers and equipment

METHOD

Make sure everything is spotlessly clean before you start, and that your refrigeration unit is working well — it will come in very handy.

Crush grapes and separate them from their stalks in a crusher–destemmer machine.

Put the crushed grapes into a press, and press out the juice (a good air bag press — one that inflates inside a steel cylinder, forcing the liquid out but leaving the skins and other stuff — is perfect).

Pump juice into a cold, closed stainless-steel tank and allow it to settle.

Add yeast.

Keep cool and allow the fermentation to proceed slowly, capturing all your grape's subtle fruity aromas and flavours.

A few days later, when fermentation has finished, pump the new wine off the 'lees' (dead yeast cells and bits of pulp that have settled on the bottom of the tank) and into another tank. Bring the temperature right down to stabilise the wine. Add a clarifying agent such as bentonite — a fine clay — to attract microscopic particles and make the wine crystal clear (this is called 'fining'). Pass the wine through filter pads so that it's bright, and bottle it.

SERVING SUGGESTIONS

Most unwooded dry white wines are sold and drunk before the next vintage comes out — or within twelve months or so of finishing fermentation. This is when they're at their fresh, fruity best.

Some unwooded whites like semillon, marsanne and riesling, however, while being delicious at this young age, also develop some tremendous toasty, rich flavours over ten or more years in bottle.

SOME OPTIONS AND VARIATIONS FOR MAKING UNWOODED WHITE WINE

Adding sugar or acid Sometimes winemakers feel the need to add what nature hasn't given them. In Old World countries like France, where ripeness can be a problem, winemakers are allowed to add sugar — a process called 'chaptalisation' — to increase the alcohol level of their wine (but they're not allowed to add acid). In Australia, where ripeness is seldom a problem, winemakers are allowed to add acid — a process called 'acidification' — to their wine to balance the riper flavours — but they're not allowed to add sugar.

Sulphur dioxide Now we could ignore the thorny topic of chemicals being thrown into wine, but we're all adults, so I think we can face up to facts. Sulphur dioxide, despite its unglamorous chemical name, is an enormously useful ingredient in winemaking, and has been for millennia. It's added in tiny amounts (measured in parts per million) at the crushing stage to almost all wines the world over, and has multiple benefits in that it prevents the juice oxidising, going brown and spoiling, kills bacteria and undesirable wild yeasts, and helps fermentation to proceed efficiently. It's most noticeable in unwooded and sweet whites,

where it can occasionally manifest itself as a smell like burnt matches. Shaking the glass vigorously with your hand over the top can help to get rid of the smell. Sulphur dioxide appears on the label under the code number 220, while a similar, anti-oxidant additive, ascorbic acid (vitamin C!), appears as 300.

Blending Winemaking is just like cooking. In both, the better the ingredients, the better the end result; in both, the idea is to capture the flavour of the raw materials and let that flavour shine; and in both, the art of blending is central.

Blending two or more different white varieties is quite common with unwooded wines, because the characters of each grape can combine in a way that increases the complexity of the end result. A good example is the blend of semillon and sauvignon blanc that I mentioned earlier. Taking herbaceous, crisp sauvignon blanc and matching it with richer, lemony semillon creates a wine that is often more attractive than the two components on their own.

It is also common to blend some unwooded wine with some that has been in contact with oak — creating a style that is halfway between the two. Blending usually takes place before the wine is stabilised and bottled.

Wooded (fuller) dry white wine

INGREDIENTS
white grapes (chardonnay is the most popular choice,
but other grapes such as semillon are also used)
yeast

EQUIPMENT
some stainless-steel equipment
oak barrels

METHOD
Follow the method for unwooded dry white
wine until the fermentation stage.

Before fermentation has finished, pump the
wine into oak barrels.

Keep the wine in the barrels to pick up some
oak flavour, making it rounder and more
complex. A normal period of time for this is six
to eight months.

Then proceed as before: pump the wine into
a tank, stabilise it, fine it, filter it and bottle it.

SERVING SUGGESTIONS
Because of the time it spends in oak, wooded
white wine is normally sold later than
unwooded. It is usually best drunk at about two
to four years old, but some of the better wooded
chardonnays develop well for many more years,
becoming very rich and honeyed.

SOME OPTIONS AND VARIATIONS FOR MAKING WOODED WHITE WINE

Which barrels? The type of oak barrel you put your white wine in has an enormous influence of the type of flavours you end up with. Brand-new barrels will give you more oaky flavour than old barrels; smaller barrels give you more oak character than big barrels; and American barrels will give you more obvious oak flavour than French barrels.

Malo makes a wine rounder and more approachable. The winemaker can decide whether the style of wine he or she is after will benefit from partial or complete malo. It is almost always encouraged in red wine, hardly ever encouraged in unwooded white, and often encouraged (and most noticeably contributes to flavour) in wooded whites.

For example, chardonnay that is fermented and aged in oak barrels is often put through malolactic, and this gives the wine its

Cleanliness is next to godliness in the white-winemaker's dictionary — and it's written in bigger, bolder, brighter letters too.

Oak chips and staves However, most of the cheaper, value-for-money wooded whites you drink wouldn't know what a barrel was if you showed it to them. A much cheaper and quicker way of giving a tank of unwooded white wine a bit of oak character is either to lower in some oak staves or to pour in a large bag of small oak chips. This gives the wine plenty of oak flavour, but tends not to contribute the complexity of barrel ageing — because the wine hasn't had the time to mellow and soften in barrel.

Malolactic fermentation Malolactic ferment-ation ('malo' or 'MLF') is a process that can take place in newly fermented wine where very crisp, hard malic acid (the acid in tart apples) is converted by bacteria to much softer, lactic acid (the acid found in milk). It can happen spontaneously, but most winemakers induce it.

characteristic creamy, buttery flavour and texture. Winemakers also commonly put only some of the barrels through the malolactic conversion, giving an element of softness that can balance well with the crisper-tasting wine that hasn't been put through malo.

Lees contact and stirring When a wine ferments, it deposits lees on the bottom of the container it's in. For unwooded and lighter styles of white, racking the wine off these lees is usual, because you want the flavours to be delicate and clean. But if you're making a style of white that's matured in barrel and more complex, that's been through malo and is big, buttery and rich, then you'll probably keep the wine in contact with the lees, too, and even stir them up from time to time, to increase complexity even more.

Wood

How red wines are made

Making white wine can be hard work, but making red wine can be *bloody* hard work. Ask anyone who, twice a day for a week, has had to punch down the solid, metre-deep cap of skins that rises to the top of a vat of fermenting shiraz. Ask them about the carbon dioxide that bubbles up from the fermenting wine, sits in an invisible, asphyxiating layer above and makes you gasp for air. Ask anyone who's had to shovel a tonne of sticky, staining, spent grape skins out of that vat when the wine has finished fermenting. And ask them about the sweaty, backbreaking grunt that is necessary to squeeze every last drop from those skins in an old-fashioned basket press.

The skin is the thing with red wine. If you get the clear juice out of red grapes and just ferment that, you end up with white wine. But if you ferment the juice and the skins of red grapes *together*, then the colour, tannins and more robust flavours in the dark skins bleed out and make the resulting wine red, too. That's where the hard work comes in — the skins don't always give up their treasure easily; it often has to be coaxed out of them.

Making red wine also tends to be muckier, warmer and woodier than making white. New red wine can cope with a bit of contact with oxygen before it's bottled — in fact, the aeration it gets as it's being pumped, pressed and racked can contribute to complexity and an ability to age well. Red wines ferment at warmer temperatures than white because this helps extract the fuller flavour and build the bigger structure required. And red wines spend more time in barrel than white for the same reason: the woody characters and rounding-out effect of oak maturation fit in with the styles being made.

Rosé
(more of a red than a white)

INGREDIENTS
red grapes (grenache and cabernet are popular choices)
yeast

EQUIPMENT
stainless-steel tanks

METHOD
Making rosé is almost identical to making unwooded dry white. The only difference comes when the grapes are crushed: if you leave the juice in contact with the red skins so that a little of the skins' pigment leeches out, you give the wine a pink blush — staining it, in other words. Apart from that, proceed as before: ferment in stainless steel, fine, filter, bottle young and drink young.

SOME OPTIONS AND VARIATIONS FOR MAKING ROSÉ
Another way of making rosé is to bleed off some of the juice in a vat of crushed red grapes soon after fermentation has started. This not only gives you a pink wine to sell as a rosé, but concentrates the colour and extract in your red wine. And yet another way — the real short-cut way — is just to add a dash of red wine to some white wine. Simple.

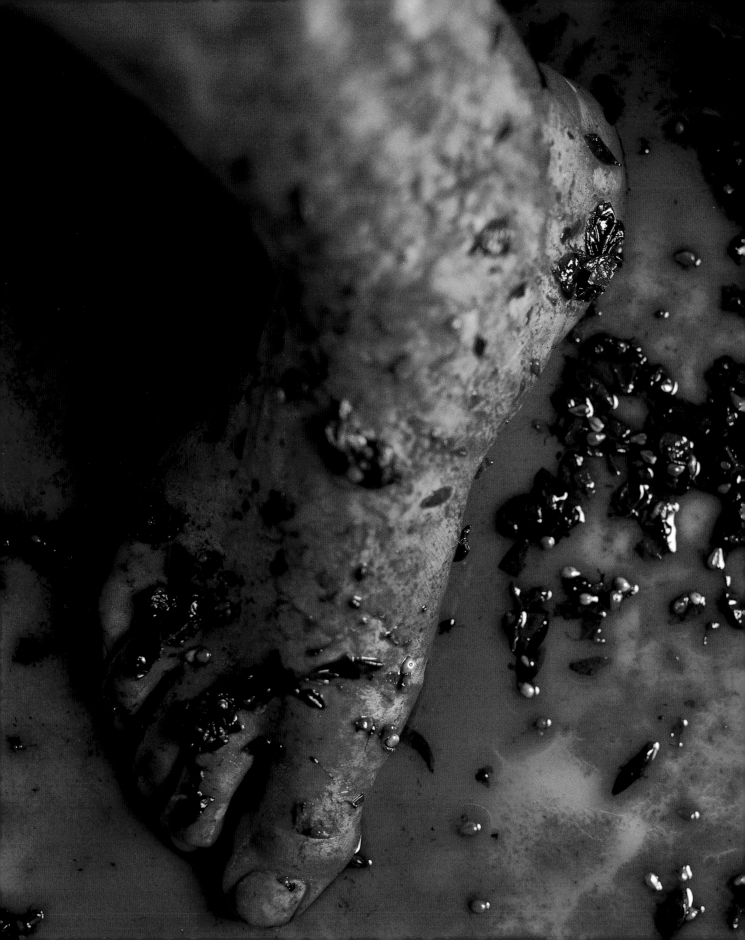

Red wine

INGREDIENTS

ripe red grapes (quite a few to choose from here, depending on the style of wine you want to make:
cabernet sauvignon, shiraz, merlot — the list goes on, but the method is essentially the same,
whichever grapes you choose)
yeast

EQUIPMENT

some big containers (concrete vats, stainless-steel tanks, etc.)
oak barrels

METHOD

Crush and destem the red grapes, and pump the juice and skins into a container.

Add yeast. While the must ferments — at a warmer temperature than white wine fermentation — make sure the juice comes into contact with the cap of skins that will rise to the top of the vat, so the all-important colour can be extracted.

When the fermentation is over, separate the glowing purple wine from the skins and pump it into barrels.

Leave the wine in barrels for nine months to a year, occasionally topping it up and racking it (transferring from one barrel to another to freshen it up and take it off its lees). The wine will go through malolactic here.

Then stabilise, filter and bottle the wine.

SERVING SUGGESTIONS

Lighter red wines are often sold and drunk like light dry whites: only twelve or eighteen months after vintage. Medium-bodied reds are usually sold and drunk at two to three years of age, and fuller-bodied reds at three to five. Modern winemaking techniques produce red wines that are delicious this young — and anyway very few people can afford or be bothered to cellar reds any more. But that's not to say today's reds, with their up-front fruit, won't age just as well as the legendary wines of yesteryear.

SOME OPTIONS AND VARIATIONS FOR
MAKING RED WINE

Whole-bunch fermentation or stalk return

Way back before clever machines like crusher–destemmers were invented, red grapes were simply chucked into a big wooden vat or pit, stems and leaves and lizards and spiders and all, and people jumped up and down on them to crush them. This worked, of course, but it often meant that the wine would extract bitter tannins from the stalks (not to mention the added protein from the beasties).

This practice still persists today, but in a slightly more controlled form. Pinot noir producers particularly, wishing to make wine in a consciously traditional manner, will either ferment some or all of their wine using the whole-bunch, stalks-on technique, or add back the stems that have been ripped off by the clever modern machine. They're after just a hint of that stalkiness from the stems to give their wine complexity and structure.

Wild yeasts

Right now, outside your front door, trillions of microscopic yeast cells are floating through the atmosphere, searching, searching, yearning to pounce on the first molecule of sugar they can find. The clever ones settle on the outside of the grapes, or in the corners of wineries, because they know that sooner or later some thirsty human will come along and crush the grapes, releasing all that sugary juice.

Until fairly recently, all wine was made relying on the wild yeasts and the wild yeasts alone, but fermentation was often unpredictable. These days, in Australia, winemakers like to be more in control, and rely on cultured yeasts — but some are returning to tradition and letting nature do its stuff. They claim that using wild (or native or natural) yeasts gives the wine more character, and the delicious results in the bottle and the glass back their argument up.

Carbonic maceration

All rules must have their exceptions, and the exception to the rule of fermentation is carbonic maceration. It's fermentation without yeast. If whole bunches of red grapes are surrounded by carbon dioxide in an enclosed space, fermentation happens inside the berries, producing wine with very fruity characters. It's a technique that is used to make light wine destined to be drunk very young, or wine that can be used to freshen a blend with fuller, more conventionally made wine.

Plunging, turning, pumping over

Sounds very tumultuous and turgid, doesn't it, like a Mills and Boon romance. But these words actually refer to the various methods of bringing fermenting red wine into as much contact as possible with the cap of skins that rises to the top of the vat.

Plunging the cap down with instruments like oversized vegie mashers frequently does the trick, as does keeping the cap submerged beneath heavy boards. Turning the cap, then pumping the liquid from below up over the top, is also good, as is fermenting in a horizontal, rotating tank, not surprisingly called a 'roto-fermenter'. But the really traditional method of taking your clothes off and jumping up and down in the vat is still employed by some winemakers with an abundance of energy. They're all techniques for getting as much flavour and extract as possible in fuller-bodied red wines.

Extended maceration And after all that plunging and turning and pumping , the wine can be left to stew for a while. This process of maceration (or leaving the new wine in contact with its skins after fermentation has finished) is applied to fuller, heavier reds, and can last for anything from a couple of days to a few weeks, depending on how much extract the winemaker wants in the wine; light reds like dolcetto, for example, might have little pumping and no extended maceration, whereas heavy reds like shiraz might have the works.

Some pinot noir producers macerate their juice with their skins before fermentation by keeping the must at a low temperature. They claim this cold maceration extracts more delicate, complex characters.

Pressings After fermentation and maceration the winemaker separates the red wine from the mass of skins by running the wine out of the vat and catching the skins in a big sieve. But this doesn't recover all the precious liquid. Oh, no. There is still a lot of wine left in and around the skins, and to get at this, they must be pressed. If the quantities are large, the skins will be pressed in a huge automated air bag or screw press, but if the quantities are only small, then a hand-operated basket press will be used. This press-wine is dark and tannic, and, depending on the style being made, is either added back to the free-run wine or kept separate.

Barrels Putting red wine into barrel to mature involves many of the same considerations as putting white wine into barrel. Brand-new barrels will give you more oaky flavour than old barrels; smaller barrels will give more oak character than big barrels; and American barrels will give more obvious oak flavour than French barrels. As already mentioned, red wines spend more time in oak than white — usually nine to eighteen months — to give them more body and structure. The exception, of course is light reds destined for young and immediate consumption, which may be left in stainless-steel tanks instead of being put into barrel at all.

Blending Again, the same principles that apply to blending white wines apply to reds, too. Some red grapes, while tasting good on their own, can taste wonderful when put together: cabernet sauvignon and merlot, for example; or shiraz and grenache.

In fact, almost all red wine you drink — and most white wine — is a blend of one kind or another. A blend of two, three, five different grape varieties; of wines from different vine-yards, or even different parts of the same vineyard, picked at different times; a blend of two different tanks of the same wine, each made in a slightly different way; a blend of five, thirty, two hundred barrels of the same wine, each of which contributes a subtle complexity to the finished product. Blending is the part of the process where the winemaker really has a chance to control the style of wine.

Fining and filtering To filter or not to filter, that is the question — whether 'tis nobler for

The skin is the thing with red wine. If you get the clear juice out of red grapes and just ferment that, you end up with white wine. But if you ferment the juice and the skins of red grapes together, then the colour, tannins and more robust flavours in the dark skins bleed out and make the resulting wine red, too.

the wine to suffer the risks of cloudiness from bacterial spoilage, or, by filtering, avoid them.

After blending, red wine is allowed to settle, and most is fined and filtered before bottling. This makes the wine stable and reduces the risk of having bacteria spoil it. It also means the wine doesn't throw a sediment to the bottom of the bottle so readily as it ages — consumers can get upset by crusty bits at the bottom of their glass. But some winemakers believe that rigorous fining and filtering also strips some of the aroma, flavour and character from the wine. So either they don't fine and they filter minimally, or they dispense with both processes altogether, relying instead on the wine falling crystal clear in the tank or barrel.

Mould
How sweet wines are made

It's hard to believe, I know, but to a winemaker intent on making great golden sweet wine, a disgusting, rotten, mouldy bunch of grapes is one of the most beautiful sights in the world. Not all sweet wines are made from rotten grapes — but the best ones are.

The rot I'm talking about isn't just any old rot, it's *Botrytis cinerea*, an airborne fungus whose minute spores weasel their way into grapes when the conditions are right (that is, coolish and humid). Botrytis isn't always a good thing; it affects some grapes more beneficially than others.

For winemakers intending to make dry whites or reds, botrytis is a pain in the neck — the fungus will viciously attack their grapes, reducing yield and making their wine taste foul and mouldy. But for a maker of sweet wine who has a vineyard full of very ripe, healthy semillon or riesling, humid, coolish conditions are something to be prayed for. Because if botrytis attacks *these* varieties, it can have the glorious effect of dehydrating the grapes, concentrating the sugar and acid substantially, and adding both glycerol (giving a luscious mouthfeel) and a particular, much-sought-after flavour to the resulting intensely sweet wine.

Sugar is the key. Theoretically, the more sugar there is in the grapes, the more alcohol there will be after fermentation. But if yeast cells work away at fermenting *very* sweet juice, the combination of alcohol and too much sugar overwhelms the cells, and they just stop working. This leaves the wine with some alcohol and some sugar — which makes it taste sweet. And the more residual sugar there is, the sweeter the wine will taste.

But as I say, botrytis-affected wines are few and far between — the ideal conditions don't come along every year. Most sweet wines are simply made with grapes that are left on the vine to be harvested later, when they have more sugar in them.

Sweet (late harvest) white wine

INGREDIENTS
very ripe white grapes (the fruitier-tasting varieties such as
riesling are usually used)
yeast

EQUIPMENT
stainless-steel containers

METHOD
Almost the same as for making dry, unwooded
white wine.

Crush and press the grapes in a cold
stainless-steel tank.

Add yeast.

Chill the wine to stop the fermentation
before all the sugar has turned to alcohol.

Stabilise, fine, filter and bottle.

SERVING SUGGESTIONS
Late-harvest wines should usually be drunk
very young, while they are fresh and fruity.

Very sweet (botrytis-affected) white wine

INGREDIENTS
very ripe, healthy white grapes (semillon, riesling and chenin
blanc are very good for this — gewürztraminer is another choice)
autumn mists
yeast

EQUIPMENT
stainless-steel containers
barrels (optional)

METHOD
Leave your grapes on the vine to ripen well.

Pray for cool, damp autumn mists to cloak
your vineyard in the morning, and for warm
afternoons to follow. Botrytis should set in and
infect your crop. If it doesn't, in some countries
(such as Australia) you can cheat and spray the
fungus on your grapes.

When the bunches are covered in mould,
pick them. (You may have to pick through your
vineyard a few times, because botrytis doesn't
attack all the grapes at once.)

Crush and press the grapes. This will be
hard, and you may have to press the
particularly shrivelled and grapes a few times
to extract their syrup. Don't be put off by the
disgusting brown appearance of the must.

Add yeast.

Fermentation will be slow, because the
yeasts have so much to do. Be patient.

When fermentation is over, put the wine into
stainless steel if it's made from one of the more
delicate varieties (riesling), and put it into oak
barrels if it's richer and more viscous (semillon).
Leave for a few months.

Stabilise the wine by chilling it down, and
fining and filtering it before bottling (very
important, as you don't want the wine to start
fermenting again in the bottle — after all, there
is an awful lot of sugar left in there).

SERVING SUGGESTIONS
Botrytised whites while being delicious young
(they are usually released at one or two years of
age), can develop over many years into sticky,
honeyed, liquid with flavours of butterscotch,
apricots, oranges, treacle . . . the range is vast.

There are a few other ways to make sweet white wines. The easiest is just to add concentrated grape juice to dry wine to sweeten it — a practice usually used for cheaper wines.

A harder way is to pick ripe grapes and dry them before pressing them — either by laying them out in the sun, or putting them on racks in an airy place. This raisins the grapes, dehydrating them and concentrating the sugar. It's a technique most often used in Italy.

An even harder way is to leave the grapes (preferably not affected by botrytis) on the vine until the cold nights of winter freeze the water in the juice. The grapes are then picked and pressed quickly, releasing the sugar-rich syrup and leaving the frozen water. This ice-wine technique, most often used in Germany, Austria and Canada, produces incredibly sweet wines, and can be reasonably well duplicated in warmer climates simply by freezing the grapes after they have been picked.

Gas
How sparkling wines are made

Cool. Cold. Ice. Making *really*, really good sparkling wine is a decidedly chilly affair.

You need grapes grown in a cool climate like Champagne in northern France or Tasmania or the Adelaide Hills or New Zealand, grapes that have ripened slowly, retaining their crisp acid and developing fine, delicate flavours. You want to ferment the juice of those grapes slowly, coldly, preserving all of its tight, citrussy deliciousness in your base wine. Then you need a cool, damp place to store the base wine, now in bottles with some yeast and sugar that will ferment and produce the bubbles. And eventually, of course, you need plenty of iced water in which to cool the bottle down before opening and pouring into suitably chilled glasses.

Seems like an awful lot of trouble to go to, doesn't it, just to make wine fizzy; you have to wonder why anyone would bother.

Because *everybody* loves a glass of gassy wine, that's why.

The image of bubbly as the anytime-anywhere-but-especially-when-there's-something-to-celebrate drink has to be the most successful marketing ploy of all time. After all, it's just wine with bubbles in it, but generations of sparkling winemakers (notably the French) have convinced us that it is somehow different, more noble than other mere table wines. Mind you, we didn't take much convincing — any excuse to legitimise having a good time. If you open a bottle of still chardonnay at breakfast people will think you're an alcoholic, but cracking a bottle of bubbly is perfectly fine (Yes, I will have just a drop more, thankyou).

There are a few different ways to put gas in wine, but the best requires heaps of time, money and effort. And quite a bit of chilling.

Top-quality sparkling wine

not overly ripe grapes (the grapes can be white or red because it's just their juice we want, not the skins)
yeast
some sugar

EQUIPMENT
stainless-steel tanks
measuring equipment for blending
heavy, thick bottles and crown seals
a cool place
time

METHOD
Press the bunches of grapes gently, without crushing them first (not surprisingly, this is called whole-bunch pressing), add yeast and ferment the fine juice to make an unwooded dry white wine. This is called the base wine. (Some top-quality sparkling wine producers aiming to make a richer style then put their base wines through malolactic and barrel maturation, but most producers avoid the malo to retain freshness.)

Make lots of other base wines. Bring out a couple of base wines you made last year and the year before.

Blend the base wines to create one final base wine that has all the elements you want for top-quality sparkling: finesse, crisp acid, length and complexity.

Put this base wine into thick bottles, add a little yeast and sugar, and seal firmly with crown seals.

Lay the bottles down in a cool place for at least eighteen months. The yeast and sugar inside the bottle will ferment again, producing a little more alcohol and lots of carbon dioxide. Because the bottle is tightly sealed, the carbon dioxide has nowhere to escape, and will remain dissolved in the wine.

The dead yeast cells will fall as lees on the inside of the bottle. Over the months, this will decompose, or autolyse, contributing a distinctive bready, yeasty flavour to the wine. But a problem arises: how to get the wine clear of these lees without losing all the gas?

The answer is to shake and turn the bottle progressively until it is standing upside-down, with the lees collected in the neck. This process is called riddling and can take weeks if done by hand but only days if done by machine. Then dip the neck in freezing brine, turn the bottle the right way up, and open the seal, forcefully disgorging the frozen plug containing the lees, and leaving the wine clear and with most of its bubbles intact. (Disgorging is done usually by machine and occasionally still by hand.)

Now top up the bottles with a mixture of a little wine and sugar — this process is called dosage — and stopper with the distinctive fat corks and wire. Leave for a few months to settle before releasing onto the market.

This is the method used in Champagne and by other winemakers elsewhere in the world attempting to make the very best sparkling wine.

Serving suggestions

Most sparkling wine is ready to drink when it's released, but some (the really good vintages and some of the better non-vintage) develop delicious, rich, almost toasty flavours if cellared for a couple of years.

An hour in a bucket filled half with ice, half with water brings a bottle of sparkling wine down to a good chilly temperature. (This will take longer in a refrigerator.) This is the best way to open a bottle of bubbly: remove the foil and wire, keeping your thumb firmly in place on the cork in case the bottle's been shaken and is itching to explode. Now cover the cork with a towel or cloth, grip this with one hand, and with the other hand, turn the bottle — not the cork. The sound you should hear on opening is a genteel *phhht*, rather than an ejaculatory bang with wine-drenching consequences. After all, the winemakers have gone to so much bother to put the gas in, it seems a shame to let it all escape at once.

SOME OPTIONS AND VARIATIONS FOR MAKING TOP-QUALITY SPARKLING WINE

The grapes You can use any grapes to make sparkling wine, but some are better than others — and cool-climate-grown chardonnay, pinot noir and pinot meunier are the best. The white chardonnay, with its finesse and length, and the red pinots, with their body and richness, combine to make top-class bubbly in a way that is unmatched by the other varieties. This is one of the only things that both Old and New World wine producers unequivocally agree on.

Although they're usually blended, chardonnay and pinot noir are sometimes made into sparkling wines on their own. Sparkling made from chardonnay alone is known as blanc de blancs (white wine from white grapes), and sparkling made from pinot noir alone is known as blanc de noirs (white wine from black . . . you've got it).

Cheaper bubblies are often made using less prestigious and cheaper grapes, such as semillon, colombard, riesling — even the juice from shiraz and grenache.

Blending Sparkling wine owes more of its particular character — not least its bubbles — to the process it goes through than it does to what grape varieties are used or where they were grown (although these do play a huge role). Almost all sparkling wines are blends of other wines, to maximise the complexity and create a certain style.

Blending a sparkling wine is a little bit like gazing into a crystal ball: you have to make a base wine with qualities that will taste good *after* it's had bubbles put in it. It takes an enormous amount of experience to be able to predict what's going to happen to the flavours in the finished product by tasting tart, green, almost undrinkable base wines.

But whether it's the extensive and very precise combining of forty different still wines made from the juice of cool-grown, premium chardonnay, pinot noir and pinot meunier for top-notch sparkling, or the slightly simpler combining of whatever comes to hand for really cheap bubbly, the idea of blending is the same.

Pink sparkling wines are made either by using red grapes and leaving the juice in contact with the skins for a while before pressing, and making the wine as if it were white, or by adding a little red wine to the blend before the second fermentation.

Vintage and non-vintage Most sparkling wine — including champagne — is non-vintage. Non-vintage wines are blends of different years, and they are made to ensure consistency of style — if one year's wine lacks acid, for example, you can blend it with last year's tart, crisp wine to balance it up and make it fit the style you want. Most top-quality Australian sparkling wine, though, and some of the most prestigious champagnes are vintage wines — the product of one vintage.

Late disgorging The longer a wine spends on its lees after the second fermentation is over and the preferred eighteen months is up, the more the decomposing yeast cells will contribute their particular bready, nutty, autolytic character to the wine. Being in contact with the yeast cells (and having an enormous amount of pent-up carbon dioxide in the bottle) also helps the wine retain its fresh, primary fruit charac-ters. So the longer the wine can stay like this, the more complex — and delicious — it will be when it's disgorged.

Economic necessity (a driving force behind many decisions in winemaking) means that most top-quality Australian sparkling is released after spending only two or — if it's lucky — three years on its lees. But occasion-ally, companies hold back a few bottles for late disgorging, and it is possible to come across wines that have had five, eight, ten years on lees. If you find any with 'late-disgorged' or a similar expression on the label, buy a bottle and taste the difference.

Other ways of making sparkling wine As I said, the method outlined above is not only the most labour- and time-intensive, but also the most expensive. The demand for sparkling wine is so great that other methods — quicker, cheaper and easier — have been devised over the years.

Transfer method — This method gets most of the same flavour as the classic method, but avoids the fuss. Base wines are put into bottles with yeast and sugar for secondary fermentation, then left in that cool place to develop all the yummy bready, nutty flavours. But instead of fiddling around with riddling and disgorging, the wine is then transferred from the bottle to a tank under pressure and filtered away from its lees. Then it's bottled, dosed (still under pressure), corked and wired.

Tank method (Also called the Charmat method after the bloke who invented it) — This method skips the riddling, the disgorging and even the bottles for the secondary fermentation. Instead, sugar and yeast are added to base wine in a pressurised tank, The secondary fermentation ensues, producing the gas, and the wine is then dosed, put into bottle (again, still under pressure), corked and wired. Quick, cheap and easy.

Carbonation — Exactly the same principle as putting the bubbles into soft drinks. A tank of base wine is injected with carbon dioxide and bottled under pressure. Quickest, cheapest, easiest. Least fun to drink.

Spirit
How fortified wines are made

When was the last time you had a glass of sherry? If the answer is 'yesterday' then give yourself a hearty pat on the back and feel very pleased with yourself. If the answer is 'can't remember' or 'never', then don't worry: join the club.

Fortified wines like sherry and muscat and port aren't exactly wetting everybody's lips these days. This is partly to do with their image. Fortifieds are seen as coming from another era, with little relevance to today. They are wines that often take decades to produce, and this is a world away from the light reds and crisp whites we all want to drink. I mean sherry's something your grandmother drank, isn't it? And liqueur muscat is something that your uncle's got a dusty crock of stashed away in the drinks cabinet. And port is consumed by bow-tie wearing, blustery, red-nosed major generals (with gout, no doubt) who remember the days of the Raj, and drink gallons of the stuff in their wood-panelled gentlemen's clubs — everybody knows *that*.

Add to these popular images a widespread niggling concern over how much alcohol we're all consuming — which makes the eighteen-to-twenty-per-cent alcohol content of most forti-fieds seem a little too strong — and it's a wonder anybody's still bothering to make them. The reason they *are*, of course, is that good fortifieds are some of the most complex and satisfying of all wine styles and there *is* still a committed, if small, market for them.

Like sparkling wine, the essential taste characters of fortified wine are derived not so much from the grape varieties used, or from where the grapes are grown, but from *how* they've been made. Fortifieds taste of the process they've been through. They taste of the strong spirit that's been added to fortify them; they taste of the long time they often spend in barrel; they taste of the slow and deliberate contact with the air that they've been subjected to.

A word about the names. Sherry, port, madeira, tokay — all these names were used by Australian producers for their various styles of fortified wine. Like champagne, claret, burgundy and chablis, they were generic names 'borrowed' a century or so ago from the original, Old World wines that the Australian versions were modelled on. The word sherry, for example, is an Anglicised version of Jerez, the southern Spanish town where most of the top Spanish sherry is made. And port is the name that was given by the British centuries ago to fortified wine shipped from the Portugese town of Oporto.

Just as with champagne, claret, and so on, the Old World wine producers wanted the Australians to stop using these borrowed names and think up some new ones of their own. The Australian winemakers agreed, and those generic Old World names are slowly going — indeed, most of them have well-and-truly gone. I just thought I would clear that up, so that you know, but I'll continue to use the old names for the sake of clarity and ease of understanding.

By the way, liqueur muscat, one of Australia's greatest fortifieds, is one wine that *won't* have to change, because it is named after the grape variety and not a wine style. Thank god for that. At least some things are simple.

Fortified wine — master recipe

There are many different styles of fortified wine, but they all begin in a similar way.

Crush some grapes and begin fermentation, exactly as you would for any wine. Then 'fortify' the wine by adding extra alcohol — either neutral spirit or brandy. This extra alcohol has two effects: it kills the yeasts and stops fermentation, and makes the resulting wine stronger than normal.

If you add the alcohol before fermentation has finished — while there is still some unfermented sugar in the juice — the fortified wine you end up with will be sweet. If you add the alcohol at a later stage — when fermentation is complete and all the sugar is gone — the finished fortified wine will be dry. What happens then depends on the style being made.

Fortified wine styles

Sherry

No other wines deserve the description 'bone-dry' as much as good dry sherries: they are the lightest, most refreshing, least alcoholic of the fortifieds, and the perfect thing to have, very well chilled, as a drink to stimulate the taste buds. At the same time, few other wines can match the complexity, heady fragrance and sheer class of good, old sweet sherries.

If you want a dry sherry, words to look out for on labels include *fino*, *flor*, *manzanilla* and *amontillado*. Sweeter sherries usually have the word *sweet* on them; and the word *oloroso* indicates that the sherry is old.

And port is consumed by bow-tie wearing, blustery, red-nosed major generals (with gout, no doubt) who remember the days of the Raj, and drink gallons of the stuff in their wood-panelled gentlemen's clubs — *everybody knows* that.

For dry sherries, a little fortifying alcohol is added after fermentation is complete, and the wine is then aged in old barrels. Because the barrels are not quite filled to the top, the sherry inside reacts with the air in the gap and partially oxidises, producing a particular nutty flavour. A strain of yeast called 'flor' is also encouraged in barrels of dry sherry, and this flor contributes a tangy, bready flavour to the wine.

Other sherries start in the same way, but more fortifying alcohol is added before they are put into barrel. The flor yeast is not encouraged and, over the many years they spend in barrel, the wines darken to a deep brown, and they develop very complex, concentrated, spicy, woody flavours.

This fine, darker, older sherry is called 'oloroso', and can be bottled dry or sweetened by the addition of concentrated grape juice. Cheaper sweet or medium-sweet sherries made in a similar way but without the years in barrel (and therefore without the complexity) are usually called 'cream' sherries.

THE SOLERA SYSTEM AND MADEIRA

Imagine a pyramid of barrels of wine of different ages, with the oldest wine on the bottom layer, and the youngest wine at the top. Each year, a portion of wine from the bottom barrels is drawn off to be bottled, and is replaced by wine from the layer above. This, in turn, is filled from the layer above that — and so on, until the top layer is reached, which itself is filled with the current vintage.

This is known as the solera system, and ensures that the wine on the bottom layer is of a consistent style, vintage variation being ironed out due to the blending and reblending process.

So if you come across a bottle labelled 'solera 1897' it means the wine inside contains a tiny portion of wine that is a century old. But you probably won't come across such a bottle: even though the solera system is widely used in Australian fortified wine production, and even though a minuscule amount of the wine in the final blends is indeed sometimes a century old, you are rarely told about it.

This system is also essential to the production of fortifieds in other parts of the world — in Spain to produce sherry, and on the Atlantic island of Madeira, where soleras of ageing fortified (called 'madeira', funnily enough) are stored in hot rooms to produce dark, burnt flavours in the wine.

PORT

The key to port — especially vintage port (port from a single year) — is very ripe, thick-skinned red grapes. In Portugal, the main variety is touriga, in Australia, shiraz and grenache are popular. You want lots of colour, tannin, flavour and sugar for this fortified wine. There are quite a few different styles of port, but the most common are vintage and tawny.

For vintage port, the grapes are crushed and fermentation is begun as it would be for dry red wine. Then, when there is still a fair amount of unfermented sugar left in the half-wine, spirit is added to stop fermentation. This takes the alcohol up to between eighteen and twenty per cent, and means the wine is sweet.

This new purple wine is then put into oak barrels for a short period (one year or so) and bottled while still deep in colour and full of flavour. Then it's left alone. Vintage port, because of its abundance of everything —

alcohol, sugar, tannin — can develop into a deliciously complex, sweet and full drink after about ten years in bottle, and continue to mellow for decades after that.

Tawny port, on the other hand, is bottled with all the ageing done for you. Tawny port is left in barrel for years — decades sometimes — to turn exactly that: tawny. The barrel ageing leaches the bold purple colour and primary fruit flavours from the wine and changes it into a much paler liquid altogether, orange–brown-coloured, nutty, woody, spicy and sometimes remarkably intense — but often a little drier than vintage port. Tawny port is usually sold as a blend of many different vintages, each contributing different characters — freshness, spiciness, and so on — to the finished wine.

Because tawny port doesn't need to be as rich and tannic as vintage port, lighter-flavoured grapes that brown quickly (such as grenache) are generally used.

You might also come across some other styles of (probably Portuguese) port. Ruby is young port blended from different vintages; late-bottled vintage is exactly that — the product of a single year that has spent a couple of years longer in barrel than proper vintage port to round out and become more approachable; vintage tawny (known in Portugal as 'colheita') is also just that — the wine of a single year that has spent ages in barrel; and again, white port is self-explanatory — port made in a similar style to ruby but using white grapes instead of red.

Muscat and tokay

These intense, sweet fortified wines (also known as 'liqueur muscat' and 'liqueur tokay',

and at their luscious best in Rutherglen, in north-east Victoria) are each made in the same way, but from different grape varieties.

Muscat grapes (to make muscat) or muscadelle grapes (to make tokay) are picked extremely ripe — sometimes with twice as much sugar as grapes used for other wines. The fortifying alcohol is added early during fermentation, when a huge amount of residual sugar is still present in the wine.

This very sweet, spiritous liquid is put into barrels — often into a solera system — and left alone, sometimes for very long periods of time. Finished muscats and tokays are always blends of different years. Very young wine contributes fresh fruitiness to those blends, middle-aged wine contributes sweetness and body, and even very tiny amounts of very old wine — sometimes a century old — contribute complexity and depth.

Muscats tend to be more exuberantly aromatic, fruity and sweet than tokays, which themselves, nevertheless, can sometimes be like liquid toffee.

Serving suggestions

The drier or younger a fortified (fino sherry, say, or vintage port) the less time you should leave it after opening the bottle because it will begin to deteriorate like any other wine; two or three days is probably a maximum. The longer a fortified has spent in barrel, acclimatising itself, as it were, to oxygen (liqueur muscat, say, or oloroso sherry), the longer you can keep it after opening without sacrificing too much freshness.

Bottle

The Enjoyment of Wine

Now for the best bit of the book — the bit about getting more pleasure out of your wine drinking. For people involved in wine for a living, like me, it's surprisingly easy to forget that pleasure is what it's all about. You can be so busy trying to remember the names of grape varieties, trying to ascertain vintage character, trying to analyse the acid levels — working, in other words — that you forget to enjoy the drink. This should never happen.

The best wines are the ones that sell out fast and get drunk and drunk and drunk and drunk — and enjoyed, with pleasure — until every last drop has gone. Wines that sit on expensive pedestals or glide through auction rooms fetching higher and higher prices until they're old, dusty and dried-out because everyone's afraid to drink them are a waste of space.

You the wine drinker are the most important part of the whole incredible process from a vine soaking up sunlight to the cork being pulled. And being a wine consumer is just like being a consumer of anything else. You can either go into the game uninformed and come away with This Month's Special Offer, faintly dissatisfied, *or* you can go in armed with a bit of understanding about what you're after — and come away with exactly what's going to give you the most pleasure.

The next few pages should help arm you with some of that understanding — or at least inspire you to find that understanding elsewhere.

Nose
Tasting wine

Learning how to taste wine — as opposed to drinking the stuff to get intoxicated — is like learning how to ride a bike. Once you've got the basic moves down, it'll come naturally to you.

Remember when you first learned how to ride a bike? Remember being uncertain about how to balance, convinced that you were never going to get the hang of it? And remember how, once you did get the hang of it, it came easily, and, after a few weeks, it felt like you'd been riding bikes all your life?

Well learning how to taste wine — as opposed to drinking the stuff to get pissed — is like learning how to ride a bike. Once you've got the basic moves down, it'll come naturally to you.

Going through the rigmarole of looking at a wine's colour, smelling it, taking a sip and really swilling it around your mouth may look stupid, but if you've spent, or are going to spend, good money on a good bottle then you owe it to yourself to try and get as much pleasure as you can out of it. Taking time over the tasting routine can help you do that.

And if you're at a winery cellar door or at a wine exhibition then going through the tasting process methodically can help you decide whether you *really* like a wine or not — after all, you should never believe all you read, especially on wine labels.

The first few times you try the four steps of wine tasting outlined on the next few pages you may feel like a bit of a punce. But after a while, you'll realise how much you gain from going through the process, and it will become instinctive. So instinctive, in fact that you might not even realise you're doing it.

Whether you're tasting a wine for the first time with a view to buying it, or you've just opened a bottle you've been keeping for years, or you're tasting a sip of the bottle you ordered in a restaurant, the principle is the same: a few seconds of concentration can really help you enjoy that wine more.

Before You Start

First of all, get yourself some good glasses. The ideal glassware for wine tasting has clear, blemish-free glass so that the wine's colour isn't distorted; a base to hold the thing with so that swirling the wine around is easy and your hand's heat doesn't affect its temperature; and a bowl that converges towards the rim, so that the wine's all-important smells are directed towards your hooter.

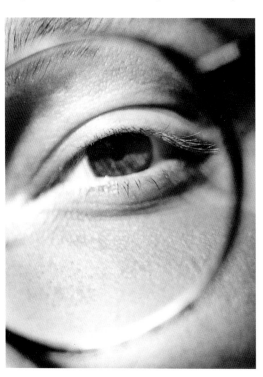

There is what's known as an international tasting glass that conforms to all these criteria, and it's fairly widely available. But it doesn't really matter if you can't get hold of one: as long as the glass you do taste out of at the very least converges towards the rim, you're better off than trying to taste out of an old chipped china mug.

In an ideal world, the perfect conditions for wine tasting are peaceful and distraction-free. They should combine some good indirect sunlight and a white surface to look at the colour of the wine, a room free of odours that could clash with the wine, silence for concentration, and a bucket, or something to spit into.

But that sounds more like a laboratory than a place of pleasure, and anyway, who lives in an ideal world? You'll seldom come across exactly that combination of conditions when you're tasting or drinking, so the best you can do is bear your environment in mind when you do taste or drink.

Squint

Right, now, you've got your glass, and you've got the wine you want to taste. The trick is to fill your glass only a third full — or even less than that — for two reasons: you'll be tilting the glass away from you to look at the wine's colour, and you don't want to lose half of the precious liquid in the process; and you'll be swirling the wine vigorously, and doing that with a full glass can be a very wet experience.

First you want to look at the wine's colour (this is where that good light and a white surface come in handy). Hold the glass by its base and tilt it away from you, until the wine almost reaches the edge of the glass.

Now look down through the wine; you should be able to see from the deepest part to the rim of the liquid. What you are looking at can tell you a hell of a lot.

For example, is the wine clear? As a very general rule, most wines are — or should be — crystal clear and bright, no matter what colour they are. And as a general rule, if a wine is clear and bright, it means the wine is in sound condition.

The colour is the next thing you look at: it gives you clues as to how old, full and perhaps how sweet the wine might be. For example, for whites, the lighter the colour, the lighter and younger the wine will probably be; for reds, the more purple the colour, the younger the wine will probably be.

I say 'probably' because, although a wine's colour can often tell you an enormous amount way before you even take a sniff, the colour can also be deceptive. Old oak-matured dry whites such as char-donnay, for example, can look just like younger sweet whites such as late-picked riesling — both a lovely gold yellow. And light-looking pale-brick-coloured pinot noir can be surpris-ingly concentrated, powerful and alcoholic in the mouth.

You may also notice some fine drops of clear liquid running down the sides of the glass after you have tilted or swirled some wines. These 'tears' (or 'legs', depending on how whimsical you feel) are a good indication of how alcoholic the wine is: the more numerous and the thicker the tears, the higher the alcohol. Some really strong wines, such as old muscats, can coat the inside of the glass in a slow-motion waterfall of thick tears.

Swirl and Sniff

It's really hotting up now; this next stage — getting a good sniff of the wine — is the most important part of the whole process.

Hold the glass upright by the base and give it a good brisk swirl. Try to make the wine circle around inside the glass, so that it almost but not quite leaps over the edge. What you're doing is breaking the surface tension of the liquid and releasing the aroma into the air.

Stop swirling, stick your nose into the glass and take a good, deep, satisfying lungful. Have a think about what you're smelling, then swirl and sniff again. You can carry on like this for as long as you like before taking a sip. In fact, with really good wines, the smell can be so delicious that you almost *forget* to drink.

The smell of a wine, its 'nose', can tell you nearly everything you need to know about it. The nose is a great indication of what grape variety the wine is made from; some varieties, like gewürztraminer, are a dead give-away on the nose, while blends of two or more grapes can be a little harder to spot.

The nose can tell you how developed the wine is; bright, perfumed, yeasty smells can indicate that the wine has recently finished fermenting, and is very young. And the nose can also give you an idea of where the wine is from; there's a characteristic eucalypt/mint smell in central Victorian shiraz, for example.

But most of all, the nose is where all the wine's complex flavours are. Flavours are smells, and smells are flavours. If the wine has smells of oak and blackcurrants and spice, then you can be pretty damn sure the wine is going to have flavours of oak and blackcurrants and spice.

Try going through this whole wine tasting process when you've got a cold, or hayfever, or a hangover, or something else that blocks your nose. You might as well be sipping dishwater. Oh, you'll *taste* the wine — as in being able to tell whether the wine *tastes* sweet, tastes *bitter* or tastes *acidic*. But try to describe the wine's all-important *flavours*, the bits that make it fun to drink, and you won't have a hope in hell.

That's why you want to have a clear nose before you take a bloody great snort of the wine in front of you: you want to drag those all-important smells to the back of your throat and up to the bulb of nerve endings inside your head that transfers those smells to your brain.

Apart from all those positive things you want to find when you swirl and sniff, also bear in mind that less pleasant pongs may be waiting for you. Many wine faults, such as cork taint, can be picked up on the nose, and that is why

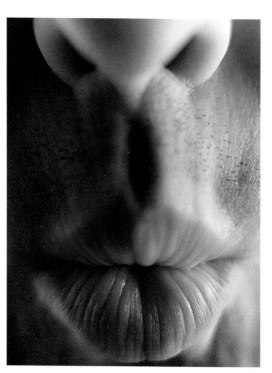

the restaurant ritual of smelling a wine before the bottle is poured exists.

Swig and Suck

Now take a small mouthful of wine — not a big gulp, but just enough to coat your tongue and fall down the sides of the gums.

Chew on the wine for a few seconds. Move the liquid around your mouth. Let the wine cover all the corners of your tastebuds.

Then (this is the bit that your friends will take the piss out of you for) tilt your head forward a little, purse your lips together and suck air across the wine to that bulb of aroma-sensitive nerves at the back of your throat. This is like smelling the wine again but from the inside.

Now you're really *tasting* the wine, on your palate. Your tongue's tastebuds will pick up the sweetness of the wine and its acid — telling you whether it is dry and crisp like an unwooded semillon (has no residual sugar left after fermentation) or really sweet like a botrytis semillon (has lots of residual sugar left after fermentation). The wine's textures are picked up here, too. That same botrytis semillon, for example, will have a fair amount of soft, velvety glycerol, giving the wine a lusciousness on the tongue. A full-bodied cabernet sauvignon's tannins will register as an astringent, dry, puckering sensation on the sides of your tongue and gums.

And then of course there's the alcohol. The good feeling that alcohol imparts is not just a reward for having gone through all this rigmarole; alcohol plays a crucial role in the flavour and structure of wine. The amount of alcohol in a wine affects how full it tastes: the lightness of a young German riesling comes in part from its ten per cent alcohol, just as the rich, heavy sweetness of a Portuguese vintage port is partly due to its twenty per cent alcohol.

Spit or Swallow

But hold on, I've left you hanging there with a mouthful of wine, haven't I? Well that's no good. You'll have to do something with it, and there are only two options open to you: spit or swallow.

If this is the only wine you're tasting, or you've only got a couple of wines to taste, then you might as well swallow what you have in your mouth. But if you're tasting more wines — at a winery cellar door, for example — then you'll get embarrassingly legless in no time, so spit it out. There's no special knack to the spitting — just try to avoid hitting anybody (including yourself). Something to spit *into* is obviously a good idea.

But it's not all over yet. You'll notice that whether you've spat or swallowed, the wine will (hopefully) have left an aftertaste lingering in your mouth and throat. This is the wine's 'finish'. Good wines have a long, lingering aftertaste, sometimes seeming to go on for minutes, not wanting to fade. Not-so-good wines tend to kind-of peter out somewhere near the back of your tongue and leave you with the impression that you never even drank them.

Smelling and tasting like this gives you a picture of the wine in your head. A good wine will paint a complete picture, be balanced, harmonious, long-tasting, and have the kind of complexity that makes you drink each glass with excitement.

And of course to really get a full picture of the wine in front of you, you have to start all over again and take another mouthful. And another, and another, and perhaps another . . .

WINE	COMMENTS
97 Riesling	- very pale, watery whi? - zesty citrus fruits and flo - very crisp, zingy wine, not
96 chardonnay (unoaked)	- pale straw - lemons and chalky char
96 chardonnay	- fruity and yeast, has a l - pale yellow gold

Babble
Words and wine

Right now, as you read this, somewhere in the world, someone is: sipping a barrel sample of young pinot noir in a dusty underground winery and describing its nuances to a visiting supermarket wine buyer; standing in front of a class full of students and explaining what makes the wine in the left-hand glass taste different from the wine in the right-hand glass; standing in a wine shop, listing the attributes of this month's special offer to a regular customer; getting very excited by the staggeringly complex array of smells in a glass of old shiraz, and sharing their excitement with everybody else at the dinner table.

Talking and reading about wine is the next best thing to actually drinking it.

I make something resembling a living out of writing about wine. I spend an inordinate amount of time thinking of words to describe fleeting flavours and subjective sensations to other people, in the hope that they might get some idea of what it's like to drink a particular drink.

Words and wine can and do have a natural affinity, and having a few handy words up your sleeve will help you describe — if only to yourself — what it is you're tasting.

Responding to wine is, at its most honest, a simple case of yum and yuck. If you like a wine, it's yummy, if you don't, it's yucky. But you'll soon find that that's not enough.

You'll stick your nose in a glass of wine one

day and it will actually smell like blackcurrants and cedar and tobacco — goddamnit, those wine writers were right after all, they weren't making it up. And you'll find yourself trying to describe these flavours to the first person you see and they'll look at you like you're crazy, but you'll know, you'll know, that there's no turning back, that you're hooked, and you'll spend the rest of your life looking for — and finding — tropical fruits and hints of toffee and barrel-ferment characters in wine after wine after wine.

So here's a list of wine words and their meanings. Use this as a reference if you come across a word on a label that sounds important and you don't know what it means. Flick through it and see if there are any words that might crystallise what you've been thinking about certain wines or styles. But you don't have to memorise the whole list. Enjoying wine isn't a test. There won't be an exam at the end of the book.

These are technical words (the nouns) that might throw some light on some of the more baffling bits of wine, and tasting words (the adjectives) that I find myself using a lot to make a wine live in somebody else's imagination.

You may ignore this bit, and be happy as a descriptor minimalist, confining your comments to 'good wine' and 'bad wine', and avoiding the jargon like the plague. But be warned. You might also find yourself turning into a jargon junkie, revelling in 'malolactic fermentation' and 'nutty autolysis' and 'excessive volatile acidity' like the proverbial pig in shit.

Wine waffle
(and what it all means)

acid   A component of grapes and wine. Despite the harsh, sour connotations of the word, acid (particularly tartaric acid) is important to the structure and balance of wine, contributing zest, life and freshness, and helping the wine age.

acidic   Zingy, crisp, fresh, lively, juicy, tangy, zesty, lemony, citrussy — these are all good synonyms for *acidic* when the acid has contributed positively to a wine's structure. Sharp, tart and sour can all be used to describe a wine with excessive or unbalanced acid.

aggressive   Wine that hits you in the mouth, that feels like it's marching up and down on your tongue in acid-heeled stilettos, or thumping your gums in with tannin sledgehammers, might be described as aggressive.

alcohol   Without it, wine would just be interesting grape juice. A funny poison, alcohol in moderation can be a wonderful thing; immoderation gives you a sore head and can do you serious damage.

aldehyde   A nutty-smelling compound produced when juice or wine comes into contact with oxygen in a controlled way. Most often used as a tasting adjective with styles such as sparkling and fortified, as in: 'My word, this old vintage champagne has wonderful, nutty, aldehydic characters!'

aperitif   The drink you drink before you're having a drink. Good aperitif wines, like sparkling wine or dry sherry, should tickle the tastebuds and leave you thirsty for more.

appellation   Geographically defined wine region. In France, where the word originated, the *appellation contrôlée* system is governed by detailed laws about what varieties can be planted where, and how wines can be made; in Australia, a much looser system is being developed, dealing just with the boundaries of a region. ('On *this* side of the road, I'm standing in the Barossa Valley wine region.' Hop. 'And on this side of the road, I'm standing in the Eden Valley wine region.')

aromatic   A catch-all phrase that refers to wines with strong positive aromas, such as the powerfully varietal smells of good sauvignon blanc.

austere   A wine that tastes a little mean, hard and tight is austere, as though the flavours are there, but the wine doesn't want to give them to you.

autolysis   Once yeast cells in bottles of sparkling wine have done their important work — causing a secondary fermentation — they die, fall to the side of the resting bottle and begin to autolyse, or decompose. After eighteen months, these autolysing cells begin to contribute a particular bready aroma to the wine, which becomes more noticeable the longer the wine spends on lees. ('My word, this late-disgorged old vintage champagne has wonderful, bready, autolytic characters!')

balanced   All of life is about balance, isn't it? Wine's part of this. A wine that is balanced has all its elements — fruit, tannin, acid, length — in seamless harmony.

barrel   Wooden container for maturing wine, almost always made from oak. Barrels come in many different sizes, with the barrique at 225 litres and hogshead at 300 litres being the most common in Australia, and different types of barrels give different flavours to wine matured in them. Brand-new barrels give you more oaky flavour than old barrels; smaller barrels give you more oak character than big barrels; and American barrels give you more obvious oak flavour than French barrels.

basket press   An upright cylinder of vertical wooden slats, bound by metal hoops, surrounding a central screw shaft. After red wine has finished fermenting and been pumped away (the free-run wine), the remaining grape skins are shovelled inside the cylinder and heavy boards are placed on top, attached to the screw. These are then slowly turned down, and the wine that was held in the skins — rich in colour and tannins — is pressed out. Depending on the style required, this press wine or pressings is added back or left out of the free-run wine.

baumé   A measure of the sugar in grapes and therefore the potential alcohol in the resultant wine. There are other measures (known as 'oechsle' or 'brix') but baumé is the most straightforward — twelve degrees baumé roughly equates to twelve per cent alcohol.

blanc de blancs   Literally white wine made from white grapes, as opposed to blanc de noirs: white wine made from red grapes. Most often applied to sparkling wine, as in, 'My word, this blanc de blancs champagne has wonderful, lemony chardonnay characters!' or, 'My word, this blanc de noirs champagne has wonderful, strawberry pinot noir characters!'

botrytis cinerea   An airborne fungus that attacks grapes in cool, humid conditions. Also known as 'noble rot', because when it infects good grape varieties such as semillon or riesling, it dehydrates the grapes, concentrating the sugar and acid substantially, and adding both glycerol (giving a luscious mouthfeel) and a particular, much-sought-after flavour to the resulting intensely sweet wine.

bottle-aged   If wines are left alone in the bottle for a number of years, they develop bottle-aged characters, quite distinct from the fresh, fruity characters they had when they were young. For most wines, this bottle age just makes them smell and taste … well, old. But some wines develop magnificent bottle-age complexity. Good dry riesling, for example, can develop a toasty and sometimes bizarre, kerosene-like aroma, and good old cabernet can develop a smell like cedar or cigar box.

buttery   Some winemaking techniques — for example, malolactic fermentation and lees contact — can contribute a rich, creamy, buttery aroma and flavour to wooded whites such as chardonnay.

carbon dioxide	A by-product of fermentation, carbon dioxide is usually left to dissipate in the atmosphere, but sometimes it is intentionally captured in bottles to make sparkling wine
carbonic maceration	Fermentation that occurs inside intact red grapes — notably the gamay grape in Beaujolais, France — producing fruity, purple-coloured wines to be drunk young.
chalky	Steely, flinty. One of many words used to describe mineral- or stone-like flavours and textures in some — especially very dry white — wines. It's perhaps too fanciful to suggest a direct link between these flavours and the mineral-rich ground the vines are grown in — but many have tried to do just that.
chaptalisation	The winemaking shortcut, outlawed in Australia, of adding sugar to grape juice to increase the eventual alcohol of the wine. (Australian winemakers *are* allowed to add concentrated grape juice to achieve similar ends.)
chewy	Think of an aggressive wine, and tone it down a notch or two. Chewy wines (usually red) are wines with lots of grape-skin extracts such as tannin, giving a strong impression of being really thick and full in the mouth.
clean	Simply, a wine that is free of faults, fresh-tasting, pleasant. Clean can occasionally be a more loaded description, implying the that the wine is technically correct, but not overly *exciting*.
closed	Or dumb. You know a wine particularly well; you've tasted it quite a few times. You open a bottle and it seems but a shadow of its former self. The wine is probably a bit closed — going through a phase between primary and secondary development, or just feeling a bit reticent. Nobody knows quite why, but it does happen. The opposite, of course is open: a wine that seems to be wearing all its flavours on its sleeve and showing off a bit.
coarse	Wine that's a bit unsubtle and rough-tasting is coarse — a bit too tannic, a bit too acidic. Unbalanced might be more correct; rustic might be more diplomatic.
complex	You take a sniff and smell blackberries. You take another sniff and smell cherries. Another and wet undergrowth. Another and just a hint of fresh cracked pepper. You taste it and it seems to fill your mouth with a basket of dark fruits, layer upon layer coating your tongue in explosions of flavour. You're not crazy; this isn't a dream. This is a complex wine.
concentrated	Seems as though the wine's flavours concentrate along the centre of your palate; often found in wines made from low yields or old vines.

decanting Pouring a wine from one vessel into another, usually to get the wine away from any sediment or crust that might have fallen to the bottom, and to allow the wine to breathe. Sediment is usually made up of tannins and pigments that, with time, have fallen out of solution (in red wine) and tartrate crystals, the solidified form of tartaric acid (in both red and white). Breathing gets rid of any bottle stink or stale odours that may have built up over time, too, and perks the wine up a bit by giving it a gentle shake.

dusty The tannins in young red wines give a bizarre impression of being dry and dusty along the sides and back of your tongue.

earthy A whole spectrum of aromas and smells fall under this word. Italian reds and older reds from quite a few places often leave a really strong impression of actually having wet clay, forest floor or sweet soil in the bottle. A good thing, too — earthy wines can be delicious.

extractive A red wine which has a little too much colour and/or tannin for its own good, so is unbalanced.

fat Self-explanatory, really: a wine that fills the mouth and sits like a lump on the palate. Not necessarily a good thing, as it indicates the wine doesn't have enough acidity to balance it up.

faults Now this could be a chapter on its own. Things can, and occasionally do, go wrong with wine at any stage from when the grapes are picked to when the bottle is opened. Whether because of the avoidable, like too much sulphur dioxide being added by the winemaker, or the unavoidable, like a tainted cork, the things listed below indicate faults in wine. If you find them in your wine, you have every right to complain, send back the bottle to the waiter, or ask for an exchange from the bottle shop.

fault 1: hazy appearance In some wines (pinot noir labelled as 'unfiltered', for example), cloudiness is perfectly okay, but in wines that should be crystal clear — a one-year-old riesling, for example — it can indicate bacterial spoilage.

fault 2: wrong colour Remember that brown is the colour of age, so if you open that one-year-old riesling — a wine that should be sunlight-bright, with flashes of green — and it's a dull ochre, this probably means the wine has oxidised (has reacted with oxygen and is on its way to becoming vinegar). While we're on appearance, it's worth mentioning that glass-like crystals in older white wine, and dark crunchy bits in older red wine are *not* faults, but natural deposits that can occur with age.

fault 3: aldehydic smells Unless, of course, you're smelling a wine that is *meant* to be aldehydic (like some fortifieds), these smells are usually unwanted and indicate the wine has oxidised. Again, if our young riesling smells like a dry sherry it's definitely faulty.

fault 4:
rotten eggs

This particularly pungent smell comes from hydrogen sulphide, which can form in a wine during fermentation. It is usually easily dealt with by the winemaker, but occasionally creeps into the bottle. Over time, it can form mercaptans, compounds that smell like burnt rubber or boiled vegies. Not to be confused with excessive sulphur dioxide, which can smell like burnt matches, and can also be a fault.

fault 5:
vinegary or
solvent smells

These come from excessive levels of volatile acidity (known as VA), and/or ethyl acetate. The volatile acids (such as the vinegar acid, acetic acid) are the ones we can smell. Ethyl acetate is formed when acetic acid combines with alcohol. A little VA can add complexity and lift the aromas of a wine; a lot can make it smell like paint stripper.

fault 6:
musty,
mouldy smells

These can occasionally be caused by the wine being stored in dirty, old barrels, but most often a musty smell is caused by the grandpappy of all wine faults: cork taint. When you think about it, the idea that wine costing sometimes hundreds of dollars a bottle is stoppered with a bit of old bark is quite odd, to say the least. That little cylinder of bark, stripped from a tree in Portugal, although boiled and sterilised, is full of tiny holes and prone to all kinds of contamination — even, perversely, contamination from the very bleach used to sterilise it! Bad cork taint, or corkiness, manifests itself as a really rank, mouldy smell and taste, but it can, at very low levels, merely dull the wine and make it taste a little flat. Estimates of how much wine is affected run between two and twelve per cent of all bottles. Many producers are experimenting with new ways to close the bottle: synthetic corks, plastic seals, even crown seals like you'd find on a beer bottle.

When they are present in excessive amounts, all these faults are pretty easy to spot. But, of course, they are rarely present in excessive amounts, and different people have different sensitivities to the various faults. For instance, I need a wine to have really obvious volatile acidity (VA) to be put off by it, whereas the person sitting next to me might be screwing up their nose at the merest hint of VA. On the other hand, I smell cork taint at a hundred paces, when everybody else has almost finished the bottle and is saying how much they enjoyed it. Remember also that one person's *minor* fault may be somebody else's distinctive and appealing character.

fermentation

The furious, frenzied, bubbling process where yeasts convert sugar to alcohol, carbon dioxide and heat.

fining and
filtering

People like to drink wine that is crystal clear and bright. This can be achieved by racking (pumping the wine off its lees) and allowing it to settle, but there is a small risk of minute bacteria and even yeasts making their way into the bottle during this process, making it hazy and causing all sorts of problems. So the vast majority of winemakers also fine and filter. Fining is the process of adding an agent such as egg white (very traditional) or bentonite clay (more modern) to pull the tiny particles out of the wine and clarify it. Filtering is done by passing the wine through a very fine filter. Purists claim that these processes also strip the wine of some of its flavour and character, so they don't fine or filter their wine, preferring complexity to stability.

firm Solid, taut, tense, sturdy — a more pleasant version of austere.

fleshy A more positive way of saying 'fat': a wine with plenty of palpable fruit in the mouth.

floral Literally smelling of flowers.

forward A wine that seems to be getting old before its time.

fragrant A wine with lifted, sometimes ethereal, light, delicate aromas.

fruity Literally, smelling strongly of fruit. But which fruit? Some grape varieties have distinctive fruit aromas associated with them — the lychees of gewürztraminer, the blackcurrant of cabernet sauvignon, for example. Some wines, especially blends of more than one grape variety, just smell broadly of 'red fruits' or 'citrus fruits'.

full-bodied a wine that fills the mouth and seems to impose on the palate — in contrast with medium- and light-bodied wines, which make a less imposing impression.

gamey Similar territory to the earthy range of smells; gamey, leathery, meaty smells and flavours often appear in older red wines.

grapey Seems obvious, doesn't it? But very few wines actually smell like grapes, with wines made from the muscat grape being a notable exception.

herbaceous There are two main reasons why a wine might smell grassy, herbaceous or green. It's either meant to — like sauvignon blanc — or the grapes that made it were under-ripe — like some red wines grown in very cool climates.

honeyed Wine showing a strong smell of honey; usually associated with older whites, especially wooded dry wines such as chardonnay, and sweeter, botrytis-affected wines.

hot Wine made from overripe grapes grown in warm climates can produce a hot-tasting burn of alcohol at the back of the throat. The fruit in those wines can also taste a bit jammy.

lees All the crap that falls to the bottom of a tank, barrel or vat of fermenting wine — the dead yeast cells, the bits of pulp, the seeds and some bits of skin and stalk. Also refers to the dead yeast cells that fall to the bottom of a bottle of sparkling wine after its secondary fermentation.

lifted Sometimes the delicate, spicy or fragrant aromas in a wine seem to be lifted towards your nose by some invisible hand. This is often volatile acidity, in its restrained and benevolent form, adding a little piquancy to the aroma.

long A very good thing. A wine that has a long finish is one whose flavours seem to go on and on and on for seconds, right down the back of your throat. The opposite, obviously, is a wine with a short finish, which is nowhere near as enjoyable.

malolactic fermentation The process that can take place in newly fermented wine where very crisp, hard malic acid (the acid found in tart apples) is converted by bacteria to much softer, lactic acid (the acid found in milk). It can happen spontaneously, but most winemakers induce it.

mildew and other diseases There are a number of diseases that the grapevine can fall prey to. The most common in Australia are the mildews (powdery and downy), which attack vines, and the rots (notably *Botrytis cinerea*), which attack grapes. These diseases occur in humid weather, and can have harmful effects on the yield and the health of the vine.

mousse The mousse is to sparkling wine what the head is to beer. A good sparkling wine should have a mousse that remains in the glass for the duration of the drink, and the bubbles that form it (called the bead) should be as small as possible. As in: 'My word, this young non-vintage champagne has a wonderful, persistent mousse and terribly fine bead!'

must After the grapes have been crushed, and before they become wine, the juice, pulp, skins and other goodies are known as 'must'.

nutty Sometimes it's because of the barrels they're stored in (chardonnay), and sometimes it's a character of the variety they're made from (pinot gris), but flavours of nuts — hazel, brazil, almond, you name it — can crop up in white wines when you least expect them.

oily Very rarely encountered, so don't worry about it too much, but occasionally, white wines — like those made from viognier or marsanne — can have a really slippery, oily texture to them that isn't at all unattractive.

oxidation You know when you cut open an apple or an eggplant and before your eyes the exposed surface goes brown? That's oxidation — the effect of oxygen on the chemicals in the food. Oxygen can have the same effect on wine; the wine slowly oxidises and goes brown and flat, eventually turning into vinegar. But in a controlled way — in the production of sherry and some sparkling wine, for example — exposure to oxygen can make the wine more complex.

phylloxera A tiny, incredibly hard-to-eradicate louse that likes to munch on the roots of grapevines (which steadily decreases the yield of the vine and eventually kills it). Phylloxera swept through Europe and much of Australia at the end of the nineteenth century, devouring vineyards as it went. Then it was discovered that American vines were immune to the louse, so now most vineyards in phylloxera-prone areas (and that means just about anywhere) are planted on American rootstocks. Phylloxera is still there, though, and ungrafted vineyards — apart from those planted in sandy soil (a habitat the louse isn't fond of) — are still at risk.

pungent More than just aromatic, pungent refers to those special moments when you come across a wine that really lets off a smell — mostly good, but sometimes not. Really good gewürztraminer and sauvignon blanc can be pungent.

rancio A quite offputting tasting term that refers to the quite delicious roasted nuts and bitter caramel smell of some very old and lovely fortified wines.

reserve Strictly should mean wine held in reserve to be released at a later date, but is used in Australia as a general indication of better-than-average quality — as are 'show reserve', 'winemaker's selection', and so on. Real reserve wines (wines reserved from previous vintages) are very important as blending components in sparkling wine production.

rich Wine with lots of viscosity, flesh, substance and fruit.

smoky Some white varieties such as gewürztraminer and pinot gris can make wines with a dusky, smoky perfume; and sometimes barrels can give wine that's stored in them a different, more pungent, smoky, charred, aroma.

soft Docile, smooth, elegant, well-balanced, mature, approachable — all different ways of saying delicious.

spicy Like smoky aromas, spicy characters can come from the grape varieties — the pepperiness of shiraz, for example — or the barrel — the clove and aniseed aromas of some (French) oak.

spritzig A fine fizz in the glass and a gentle prickle on the tongue indicating that small amounts of carbon dioxide were dissolved in the wine when it was bottled.

stalky A little stalkiness (in wines that have been fermented with a few of the grape stems included) can be a good, complex thing. A lot just makes the wine taste green and stalky.

sulphur Sulphur has been used as a winemaking additive to prevent oxidation for thousands of years. Sulphur candles used to be burned inside barrels to build up a layer of sulphur dioxide. Now, sulphur dioxide is added to the wine in powdered form. Another sulphur compound, copper sulphate, is used in the vineyard against mildew in the form of Bordeaux mixture, the characteristic blue spray used by many gardeners on fruit trees.

tannin Make yourself a nice pot of tea. Let it stew until it's cold and almost black, then pour a cup, and don't add anything to it. Now take a sip. It will taste disgusting, but, more importantly, you'll feel like your gums and the sides of your mouth are being sucked through the taste buds on your tongue. This puckering astringency is caused by the tannins in the tea — and these tannins are also found in grape skins and stalks. Red wines are usually high in tannin (described as being very tannic) if they are made from grapes with thick skins, or have had extensive maceration or some contact with stalks during fermentation. Tannins can also leach out of oak barrels into the wine stored in them.

terroir How the unique combination of soil, slope, sunlight, and so on in a vineyard affects the taste of the resulting wine. For the French, the idea of *terroir* is traditional and sacrosanct ('This wine tastes of its *terroir*'.) New World winemakers, on the other hand, are only slowly coming to terms with the concept.

thin The opposite of fat, and hardly ever a good thing. Thin wines, wines that are really neutral-tasting, that seem hollow and lean, are usually the result of overcropped grapes and poor winemaking.

ullage Given the chance, wine likes to evaporate if it's kept hanging around. It will evaporate through the cracks and loosely sealed bungs of a barrel, and it will leak and evaporate through a contracting and expanding cork in a bottle. The space that's left in the barrel and the bottle is called the ullage. Barrels can be topped up, as can very old, precious bottles — by having their corks taken out and the space filled with a younger vintage of the same wine. But most bottles are left to ullage away over the years. Badly ullaged wines, whose levels have fallen below the shoulder of the bottle, tend to oxidise as well, but a little ullage is not necessarily so harmful.

variety/varietal Two words which are often confused. A grape *variety* is a type of grape. A varietal wine is a wine made from one variety. (Varietal is also used as a tasting term to describe a wine that smells and tastes varietally correct — blackcurranty cabernet, for example; or peppery shiraz.)

velvety Wine which is seamless, balanced and has a smooth, supple texture in the mouth. Often applied to good pinot noir.

vinous Just like the word *grapey*, you'd think a word that means 'wine-like' would crop up more often in wine tasting, wouldn't you? Funnily enough, it's hardly ever used.

viticulture The practice of growing vines — in this case, the grapevine, and in particular, the wine grapevine, *Vitis vinifera*. People who do it are called 'viticulturists'. As the wine world looks harder at growing better grapes, 'viticulturists' are a crop of specialists you may well hear more about.

woody Again, a catch-all term that covers all sorts of descriptions from the vanilla-like smell of new oak barrels to the cedarwood smell of old cabernet, and also covering the toasty smells, the spicy smells, the dusty smells and even the dirty old barrel smells.

yeast There are micro organisms and there are micro organisms. Amoeba, for example, aren't much fun on the whole. But yeast — ah, *there's* a different culture of cells altogether. Yeast is the key that unlocks the intoxicating secret of the sugar in grape juice — it's the yeast cells, already in the air or introduced by the winemaker, that convert that sugar into alcohol, carbon dioxide and heat. Without yeast, wine wouldn't be nearly as much fun.

Cash
Buying wine

Shops

I've thought about it and thought about it and thought about it, and I honestly can't for the life of me think of anything that is as enjoyably time consuming as buying wine.

I can spend hours in a good record shop, and a whole morning in a good bookshop, but I can spend *days* in a good wine shop.

There's something totally absorbing about browsing in a place that's stuffed to the gills with delicious wine. All those *bottles*. Just a short yank of the corkscrew separates you and the contents of any of them (with an outlay of money in between).

My favourite wine shop is located near public transport, has good parking facilities and, best of all, is within walking distance of my house. It's spacious, with seductive lighting and well-designed display areas that are conducive to browsing: lots of nooks and crannies, even a walk-down cellar where the really precious bottles are kept. The shop is air-conditioned, the wine on display is kept in racks, lying down, and there are large temperature- and humidity-controlled storage facilities for the rest of the bottles out the back (all very important for keeping the wine in the best possible nick).

The staff are knowledgeable, friendly and can communicate well about wine — and have got to know what my particular tastes are so that they can recommend new wines they think I might like. The people who run the shop go out of their way to source interesting, little-known and great-value wines, as well as having a consistent, diverse range of reliable producers. They hold regular tastings in a light, airy room above the shop, using good glasses and inviting guest winemakers to come and show their wines. There is a regular newsletter and wine list, which is sent to customers, and the shop offers a host of services such as free delivery, glass hire, special offers, mixed cases . . .

Needless to say, this shop doesn't exist. You probably know one with good staff, but terrible storage facilities; great displays but clueless staff; that's a great shop but is difficult to get to; that holds tastings but serves the wine in plastic, thimble-sized cups.

Keep searching until you do find a wine shop that has as many of these qualities as possible — and when you do, tell all your friends. A shop like this might not be as cheap as the big, impersonal discount liquor barns, or as convenient as supermarket liquor departments, but it is going to be a lot more fun. And I strongly believe that paying a little bit extra for the little extras is worth it.

You are the most important part of the wine-buying process. You are the one who makes the final decision about whether to buy a particular wine. So try to do as much homework as possible before going out there and searching for that perfect bottle. Read wine books and articles. Browse through the hundreds of wine sites on the Internet. Write down the names of wines, styles, grape varieties and producers you like, and stash them away for future reference. If you know exactly what you're looking for, and if you know a bit about the subject, it's harder to be swayed by intimidating sales people trying to flog the latest discounted special offer.

Look for familiar and preferred names and styles, but be open-minded about trying unfamiliar and unusual wines. Give yourself a price limit and try to stick to it — knowing full well that you'll probably blow it by a couple of dollars. (You'll probably find that your price limit creeps up gradually over the years as you realise the more expensive bottles do indeed usually taste better.) Buying by the dozen is often slightly cheaper than buying by the bottle. But be cautious of huge discounts — it can mean the wine is from a not-so-good vintage, or has been stored badly and is at the end of its tether. Having said that, if you do uncover an absolute gem in the 'reduced to clear' bin, go back and buy as much as you can.

Look out for signs that the wine may have been stored badly and might not be in good condition. Weeping corks and badly ullaged bottles (where the level of wine is way below the cork) are dead giveaways. Even if you buy a sound-looking bottle, open it and find that it's faulty, don't be afraid to take the wine back, because the shop is obliged to replace it or refund your money. (But don't drink two-thirds of the bottle just to make sure it really *is* corked or has oxidised or whatever — take it back as full as possible). It's been said a squillion times before, but life really is far too short to drink bad wine.

Most of all, try to taste before you buy. Shops often hold regular tastings in-store, and every year there seem to be more and more tasting exhibitions, wine dinners, and wine shows on offer. These tastings — sometimes free, sometimes with a small charge, sometimes, in the case of the more extravagant dinners, quite pricey — are a perfect way to find the wines you really like. They are usually advertised in papers and magazines, so keep your eyes peeled. Again, if you do come across the best wine you've ever tasted and want to buy a truckload, remember to write the name and vintage down. It's so easy to think, 'Oh, I'll remember this tomorrow,' but if you're like me you won't.

Cellar Door

Winery cellar doors are the ultimate in try before you buy. Most wineries (except the ones with very small productions or very high ideas about themselves, which are open by appointment only) have tasting areas open to the public most days of the week. These cellar doors are great for a number of reasons: you can taste the wines before you buy them, you can often get wines that are unavailable anywhere else, and you can sometimes pester the winemaker — even take a look at the winery — and find out exactly why that chardonnay you tasted the last time you were here tasted the way it did.

Tasting and buying wine at cellar door is a little different from browsing in a wine shop. Here are a few tips on how to get as much out of it as possible.

For a start, very few wineries are located anywhere near public transport, so you're going to have to get there by car. And going by car means being very careful about what you drink. Take a few friends and bribe somebody to be the non-drinking driver (they get a turn to be the taster next time you go). Decide which wineries you want to visit and stick to them (four or five is a sensible number) but be prepared to be seduced by particularly intriguing dirt road turn-offs to obscure wineries.

Try to avoid strong aftershave or perfume, as fragrances not only obscure the smell of the wine you're trying, but can really get up the nose of the person behind the counter.

Don't be afraid to ask as many questions as you want. The people who work in cellar door are likely to be as knowledgeable about wine as almost anybody — certainly about the wine they're selling. They're usually quite friendly, too.

And don't be afraid to spit! Cellar doors usually provide lots of buckets, vases or even glamorous spittoons for this very purpose, so it's the perfect opportunity to really practise your squint, swirl, sniff, suck and spit. Besides, drinking a tasting amount of five or ten wines at four or five wineries is like downing a whole bottle or more — real sore-head territory.

Bear in mind that you're not under any compulsion to buy at cellar door — but neither are the tastings offered entirely out of the goodness of the winemaker's heart. You should buy a bottle only if you genuinely like the wine, but if you're not going to buy a bottle, don't shuffle around in embarrassment, just be polite.

Put your name down on any mailing list you see. Although this will mean even more paper shoved through your letter box each year, some

Mail Order, Wine Clubs and Wine on the Internet

Remote services are booming at the moment because they're so downright convenient. What could be easier than browsing through a catalogue and phoning through your order, or sitting at your computer and typing in your details, then waiting a week or so, and receiving

winery newsletters not only entertain and inform, but they also occasionally offer wines that cannot be bought elsewhere.

Auctions

Auctions are increasingly commonplace and accessible, and the auction market is becoming more dynamic. They are often conducted by silent bid (you post or fax your bid and the highest one wins), with the wines that you succeed in buying being sent to you by post. Auctions can be a great place to buy wine — and not just the expensive, rare, and the very old either. It's often possible to find current or very recent release wines listed in an auction catalogue for less than the price you would pay at the bottle shop down the road.

Again, decide on a price limit and try to stick to it — especially if it's a live auction, where the excitement of bidding against another person can force the price up dramatically — and always remember that there will be a buyer's premium and possibly sales tax added on top of the bid you make. Auctions, incidentally, are the only legal way for the public to sell wine.

a case of wine in the post?

These services often provide access to good-value wines, and they're very useful for people who live miles away from the nearest shop. But they have one major drawback — you can't taste before you buy. And you miss out on the physical involvement of browsing, of picking up bottles, of checking for signs that the wine may be past its prime. So, in other words, they're convenient, but not very much fun.

Restaurants

One of the reasons wine has become such a popular drink is its increasing presence in, and widening accessibility through, restaurants — and cafés and bars and bistros.

Buying wine in restaurants isn't as budget-damaging as it used to be. There is still the odd stuffy restaurant that seems to think of a number and quadruple it when pricing its wine list, coming up with figures that bear no relation to common sense, but that approach is dying out. Most new places are offering lighter, better-value food, and their wine lists follow suit.

More and more places are also offering a wide selection of wines by the glass, often suggesting particular wines with particular dishes. This is a great thing: it means you can try new and different tastes, and don't have to splash out on a whole bottle. But it only works if the restaurant has a high turnover of those wines served by the glass, so that bottles don't stand half full for days on end.

Of course, if you do get a glass or a bottle of wine that tastes faulty in any way, you should send it back and get a replacement (life is too short, after all . . .) That's what the much-parodied ritual of ordering and tasting is all about.

Once you've chosen your wine (and listen to advice from the waiters — if they're taking the trouble to give it, they might know what they're talking about), the waiter should bring the bottle or glass to your table and give you a chance to swirl, sniff and taste. If the wine doesn't have any obvious faults then go ahead and drink it. But If it does have a fault, then say so — politely, of course. It's your money you're spending, after all.

It's been said a squillion times before, but life really is far too short to drink bad wine.

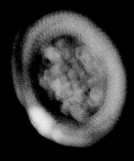

Space
Keeping wine

It's the middle of summer. You buy a couple of bottles of wine at a winery cellar door and put them in the back of the car. You visit another couple of wineries — all down particularly bumpy dirt roads. The temperature in the car gets up to forty-five degrees every time you get out and turn the air-conditioning off. Then it's a long drive back to the city.

By the time you get home, you've forgotten that the bottles are in the car. In fact you don't remember until you hear them clinking around under the old chip wrappers and parking tickets a week later. You pull the bottles out, take them upstairs to your apartment and leave them on the kitchen table until the next day.

Like thousands of other people, you've got one of those fold-out wooden six-bottle wine racks wedged in the space between the top of the fridge and a cupboard that's too high to reach without standing on a chair. You put your two precious bottles in the rack and promise yourself that you'll open them for a special

occasion. Anyway, it says on the back label that this particular wine benefits from a few years' cellaring.

Two years later, you're having a few friends over for dinner. You remember about that wine you bought, and with memories of a happy, distant summer flooding back, you carefully pull out one of the bottles from the rack . . .

Tragedy. You've pulled the cork, poured a glass, taken a sniff and it's made you almost want to cry. This wine, which tasted so good two years ago, now tastes like vinegar. And it's because of the way you treated it. The poor wine never really had a chance.

Wine's enemies are strong light, excessive heat, dryness and dramatic fluctuations in temperature — most of which the bottles in this case were subjected to. Wine likes darkness, coolness, a little humidity and, above all, a constant temperature. That's why the cellar of popular imagination — damp, candle-lit, musty, chilly, full of dusty bottles — is actually an excellent place to keep wine.

Darkness is preferable because strong light can give wine off, flat flavours (that's why most wine, especially red, is bottled in dark glass). Cool temperatures are good because extreme heat over a long period can literally cook a wine, giving it a fat, blousy, jammy . . . cooked flavour. And humidity is good for keeping the cork moist so that it doesn't dry and contract, allowing air into the bottle (this is also why bottles should be stored lying on their sides, with the wine in constant contact with the cork).

But a constant temperature (ideally around thirteen degrees Celsius) is the most important consideration of all. Frequent fluctuations in temperature make the corks even more likely to contract and expand, pulling air into the bottle and pushing wine out. This leads to tell-tale weeping around the sides of the cork, a sticky indication that the wine inside may have oxidised and be on the way to turning into vinegar.

Now, if you actually have a cellar under your house, then you're laughing; you should be able to keep wine under the best conditions for a number of years and enjoy it as it gets older. But for most of us, it's practically impossible to satisfy all these conditions, so we have to make do with compromises.

Old milk crates swaddled in towels at the back of a cupboard; recycled polystyrene wine-mailing packs stacked in a brick laundry behind the house; cardboard whisky cases crammed under the stairs; floorboards ripped up and holes dug in the ground — the ingenuity born of desperation is endless when it comes to storing wine in the cellarless home.

Solutions like these are adequate for short-term storage — say, a couple of years or so — but if you're really bitten by the wine bug and get it into your head to start collecting every vintage of your favourite cabernet, or regularly buying by the case, or laying down some vintage port for your sister's daughter to drink when she turns twenty-one, then you would also be wise to organise more efficient cellaring. You could talk to your local wine shop: they may be able to recommend a professional cellaring or warehousing service. You could splash out on an expensive temperature/humidity-controlled cabinet, or an even more costly large hole in the ground. Or you could join the rest of us scanning the property pages and dreaming of a mansion with a real cellar.

Old milk crates swaddled in towels at the back of a cupboard; recycled polystyrene wine-mailing packs stacked in a brick laundry behind the house; cardboard whisky cases crammed under the stairs; floorboards ripped up and holes dug in the ground — the ingenuity born of desperation is endless when it comes to storing wine in the cellarless home.

AN 1947

Ye Olde
Selected Hock

YERIN

VICTORIAN ASSOCIATED VINEYARDS

Time
Older wine

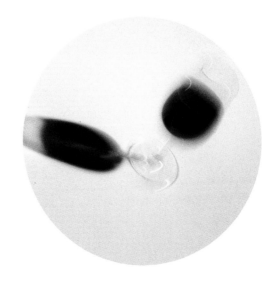

Not all wine gets better with time. Most of it is made to be drunk as young and fresh as possible, probably with food, probably not too far from the vineyards it started life in. In this respect, the vast majority of the world's wine is like the vast majority of the world's television: everyday stuff, consumed without much thought by people who just want to relax after a hard day's work. But there *is* a tiny proportion of the world's wine that not only deserves a little more attention but also can get better with time.

If you believe the statistics (and I'm disinclined to believe statistics), this chapter is irrelevant to a modern wine drinker. The figures say that well over ninety per cent of all wine is drunk within forty-eight hours of being bought. Nobody's keeping wine any more, apparently; nobody appreciates the pleasures of a fine old wine, so I might as well finish this chapter right here. For that matter, the last chapter's not much use to anybody, either, if nobody's bothering to store wine for any length of time to appreciate it when it's mature.

But I'm not going to stop, because you will, one day, if it hasn't happened already, stumble across an older wine that will not only sing sweet songs on your tongue but leave you with a deep respect for the pleasure of a good mature bottle. It might happen in a restaurant or at cellar door where the keeping has been done for you. It might happen at a friend's place, or at a tasting or winery dinner. But it will happen, and you'll be hooked, and then you'll step over into the two or three per cent of people who sometimes like to wait a little longer than a couple of days before ripping out the cork.

And then you'll definitely think about a cellar.

Older White

What do semillon, riesling and chenin blanc have in common? They can all make white wines that get better with age. I've already sung the praises of unwooded semillon — starting life as a lemony, tart young thing and ageing over the years into a rich, toasty number — but I could also, while I was at it, have told you that riesling and chenin blanc can behave in a similar way. And all three varieties, when affected by the noble rot, *Botrytis cinerea*, produce sweet whites that can age for even longer, getting ever more luscious with the passing years.

It's the acid. As dry young wines, these varietals have relatively high levels of acid, which acts as a kind of preservative (meaning the wine ages slowly, slowly turning from a pale, watery white to deep golden–yellow very gradually). That acid also combines with the alcohol in minute quantities to produce new, complex aromas as the initial fruit aromas dissipate.

This is where chardonnay's apparent supremacy in every other field comes unstuck. With notable (expensive) exceptions, chardonnay, because of its lower acid, barrel-ageing and more immediate flavours, doesn't usually age in bottle as well as the other, less popular varieties. In fact, it's generally at its best within two to four years of being released for sale.

But these explanations for how wines

form long conga chains and dance themselves out of solution. This makes the wine grow progressively paler, moving from purple to red to brick to orange–brown in colour. (This is why a red wine's colour can tell us so much about how old — or rather at what stage of maturity — it is). This is also why old red wines can have a layer of sediment at the bottom of the bottle.

These chemical changes also alter the aromas, flavours and structure of the wine. Sweet fruit aromas diminish, to be replaced by more savoury, earthy smells, and the tannins in the wine seem to become softer. That's why bigger wines like cabernet sauvignon, shiraz and nebbiolo — wines with plenty of tannin and extract in them to start with — tend to be the ones that can age for longest.

You may have read a phrase similar to 'This wine will reach optimum maturity after five years in the cellar' on countless back labels.

change over the years are only part of the answer. The fact is that science can tell us what the atmosphere is like on Jupiter but can't fully explain why wine ages the way it does.

Older Red

It's easier to see the physical effects of time on red wine than on white.

All reds start life with a blueish–purple colour. This comes from the dark colour and flavour compounds and tannins that have been sucked out of the red grape skins during the winemaking. As the wine ages, these molecules

Nobody's keeping wine any

more, apparently; nobody

appreciates the pleasures of

a fine old wine, so I might

as well finish this chapter

right here.

This doesn't mean that at the stroke of twelve on the night of its fifth birthday the wine will suddenly be at its best to drink. What it means is that the winemaker reckons that at around five years of age — and then probably for a few years after that — the balance of fruit flavours and developing bottle-aged characters in the wine will make it most enjoyable.

But that's what the winemaker reckons. If, with a bit of tasting experience you discover that you love to drink cabernet when it's young, tannic and full of bold primary fruit, then that's when you should drink cabernet. Likewise, if you prefer twenty-year-old cabernet that has lost its primary fruit but developed delicate, cedary aromas, then you should drink cabernet when it's twenty years old.

A word about bottles. There are quite a few stories about why wine is normally sold in 750-ml bottles, but my favourite explanation is that three-quarters of a litre is how much the average peasant in ye olden days would happily consume with *each* meal.

Today, of course, one 750-ml bottle is about the upper limit of sensible consumption for *two* people for the *whole day*, but it's by no means the only sized bottle you can get. Magnums (the equivalent of two bottles), double magnums and larger bottles are particularly favoured by winemakers who have wines they think will age, because the larger the container, the more slowly the wine develops.

It is generally believed that the small amount of air trapped in the bottle between the wine and the cork helps to change the flavour of the wine slowly over time. So with bigger bottles, where the ratio of wine to trapped air is larger, the rate of ageing is slower, and, conversely, the smaller the bottle (half bottles and those little fellers you see on planes) the faster the rate of ageing.

On top of that, a magnum is also a much more convivial size for a wine bottle. In fact, I reckon all wine should be bottled in magnums.

Breathe

Serving wine

In a group of thirsty people, the sound of a cork popping is guaranteed to make at least one of them break out in a broad smile. That sound, the explosive bang of air as another little plug of bark is released from its tight moorings, is enough to set *my* taste buds quivering every time.

This is the part we've all been waiting for. This is the moment of truth. This is where we get to open some bottles and drink some wine. So let's savour the moment. Let's break it down, take everything slowly, carefully, and look at how to get the most enjoyment out of the whole affair.

... serve at room temperature ...

And which room might that be, exactly? A hot bedroom in Darwin in mid-summer? A Hobart kitchen in mid-winter? A beach hut in Margaret River in the middle of a storm? Why can't those back labels be a little more precise?

How cold or warm the wine is when you drink it will affect how it tastes, but you don't need to rush around with a thermometer and a list of 'perfect' serving temperatures — rough guides are enough.

As a rule, the colder a wine, the more the hard, woody characters stand out, and the warmer a wine, the more the sweet, fruity flavours are emphasised. So drink a heavily oaked chardonnay at the ice-cold-beer temperature of most Aussie fridges and all

Darwin knows that, in summer, red wine sometimes benefits from half an hour in the fridge to bring it down to an enjoyable temperature. Common sense, really.

you'll taste is wood and acid — the wine will appear to have lost its fruit. Drink a big shiraz at blood heat and it'll be like drinking blackberry jam — the wine will appear to have lost its structure.

That leads to a general guide: the lighter, fresher and less wooded the wine, the cooler you should drink it. The fuller, more complex, and more oak-influenced the wine, the closer you drink it to that comfortable non-temperature called 'room temperature'.

Unwooded wines such as crisp rieslings, sparkling wines, seafood whites, medium-sweet whites, dry sherry and rosés can all take a couple of hours in the fridge (depending of course on how warm they are before they go in). Older whites, sweet whites, oaked whites like chardonnay, sparkling reds, even light reds such as young pinot noir can take half an hour or so in the fridge. And fuller-bodied reds and sweet fortifieds should normally never see the inside of a fridge.

But personal experience is probably the best guide of all. Somebody lucky enough to have a cool, damp cellar under an old Victorian house in Melbourne soon learns that in the middle of winter red wines have to be brought up and left in a warm kitchen for a couple of hours before being drunk, or they're just too cold to enjoy. Likewise, somebody in a modern apartment in

. . .

decant before serving and allow to breathe …

Get a pen and cross out the word 'decant' in that line. Now write above it: 'pour into a big jug'. You don't need expensive cut-crystal decanters for this bit, even if they do look good next to your Austrian glassware and Italian corkscrew. All you need is something to put the wine into — and a jug is good enough for that.

There are three good reasons for pouring wine into a big jug or a decanter before drinking it. The first is to separate the clear wine from any grit or sediment. The second is that the process brings the wine into contact with oxygen — lets it breathe — helping mellow out young reds and giving a bit of life to older reds that have got all stiff over the years (white wines seldom benefit from breathing). And the other reason is that, like other harmless rituals, it's fun.

You've got an old bottle of cabernet that your parents gave you a decade ago. You've been keeping it lying down in the cool and the dark all these years, and now's the time to open it. Bring it out of its treasured hiding place and stand it up for a few hours, to let the sediment it has thrown drop to the bottom of the bottle.

Now dim the lights, put on some good music, light a candle and put it on a table at about waist height. You could do this with an upturned torch

(with someone to hold it at the right height!) but there's something romantic about candles. This is a ritual, remember.

Make sure the jug you're going to pour into is clean, odourless, and big enough to take the contents of the bottle you're about to pour into it. Take the jug firmly in one hand while you grab your precious bottle in the other. Approach the candle and stand so you're looking down on the flame. Now pour the wine in one slow, smooth motion into the jug. Look down on the neck of the bottle and you'll see the candle flame shining through the wine as it pours through. When you see the sediment begin to rush towards

the neck, stop pouring. That's it. You now have a jug full of clear, aerated wine, and a small amount of scungy deposit that you can strain and chuck in a sauce or marinate a steak with.

Some people think that letting a wine breathe like this *is* a waste of time. I don't agree. Just pulling the cork out and letting the wine stand there is a waste of time, because you're not getting the wine into contact with much air. But I reckon the act of pouring old reds out of their bottles more often than not does them the world of good. It opens up the flavours, rounds the wine out, allows some of the off-smells that have collected in the bottle to dissipate.

The only way is to try it yourself. If you then think pouring and breathing is neither fun nor beneficial to the flavours of the wine, don't do it. But in the meantime, pass me that jug, would you?

... pour a small amount into a glass ...

If you were just drinking wine to get drunk, you'd have skipped the last bit about rituals and breathing and jugs, and just poured the stuff down your throat. Then again, if you were only drinking wine to get drunk you probably wouldn't be reading this book in the first place.

If you do just pour it down your throat then you're missing out on wine's greatest pleasure: its smell and its flavour. The shape of your wine glass can have an enormous effect on how you pick up a wine's flavours, and as I said, the best glass for really tasting — for trying new wines, for comparing one wine with another — is the international standard tasting glass. Not surprisingly, this is also a pretty good glass for drinking out of, but it's by no means the only one that does the trick.

As long as it doesn't leak, any glass will do to drink wine from. Hard-wearing tumblers and thick-glassed goblets are great for everyday drinking, barbecues and picnics because you're likely to be drinking everyday wines which you don't need to think about too much. But if you're drinking something special (that is, something you or someone else paid a lot of money for) then you want to drink it out of a glass that is going to show it to its best advantage.

Tall, narrow flutes, for example, are the best thing for good sparkling wine because they don't let all the bubbles escape at once, as wider glasses do, and they concentrate the delicate aromas. Big, goldfish-bowl-sized glasses are great for older or more complex reds because they allow you more room to swirl the liquid round to release all the delicious smells.

Again, the best way to find out which glasses you prefer for which wines is to try some combinations out yourself. Buy a bottle, pour it into a few different glasses and see which you like best. But whichever glass you plump for, try not to fill it more than half full. Try swirling a glass that's fuller and you'll end up wearing the wine, not drinking it.

Belly
Food and wine

This is how it used to be. You sat at a starched white tablecloth, and in front of you was a forest of cutlery and glasses, shimmering in the golden candlelight. Over the next few hours a series of dishes was brought out by gliding butlers, and you worked your way through the cutlery from the outside, knowing what each peculiarly shaped fork and knife was used for. And with each dish came a new wine, poured into one of the countless cut-crystal glasses. Champagne to start, sherry with the soup, chablis with the oysters, burgundy with the offal, claret with the roast beef, sauternes with dessert, port with the stilton and cognac with the cigars. The conversation tinkled and your guests went home full and happy. You never dreamed of doing things any other way.

This is also how it used to be. On the weathered wooden table in front of you was an earthen-ware bowl, an old spoon and a thick glass tumbler. You helped yourself to pasta from the big pot in the centre of the table, poured your-self some rough red wine from a big bottle with no label, took a swig and poured yourself some more. When the pasta was gone, you dribbled a little of the wine into the bottom of your bowl, tore off a big hunk of hard, crusty bread and mopped up the juices. Dessert was a couple of fresh figs and a chunk of milky cheese, washed down with more of the red and followed by a cigarette and a shot of grappa. Everything in this meal came from your farm or neighbouring farms. You never dreamed of doing things any other way.

And this is also how it used to be. It didn't matter what was on the table in front of you. It could be prawn cocktail, leg of lamb or lamingtons, the important thing was that there was not a bottle of wine to be seen. Tea, beer, water, spirits even, but not wine. The idea that wine should be a natural fixture of every meal, the sensible and instinctive accompaniment to food, was ridiculous in the majority of Australian households as recently as a generation ago. The idea that certain wines might go particularly well with certain foods didn't even enter into the equation. And you never dreamed of doing things any other way.

This is how it is today. On the table in front of you there could be a plate of char-grilled kangaroo with polenta or a bowl of Thai green chicken curry or a fresh goat's cheese or a rich chocolate cake. You could be at home alone or in a restaurant by the beach with a bunch of friends. It might be a quick lunch or a full-on birthday dinner. What is certain is that there's probably a bottle of wine on the table too (and it's probably a bottle of chardonnay).

Today we take for granted the idea of wine as a natural part of everyday life. And because wine is now commonplace, we've had to re-assess the official rules about food and wine. Some classic pairings have come out unscathed. Some of the old stuffy dictums have been laid to rest forever. And some new approaches to the endlessly pleasurable pastime of eating and drinking have emerged.

Matching food and wine isn't about finding the holy gastronomic grail. It's not about laying down rules. It's about enjoying yourself by eating well and drinking well. If you come across sublime flavour marriages that explode on your tongue, then that's fantastic — but just experimenting can be a lot of fun, too.

One of the main reasons for throwing out some of the old formal ideas about which food goes with which wine in which order is that hardly anybody eats in a formal way any more. When was the last time you sat down to soup, then fish, then poultry, then meat, then cheese, then dessert? Most of our meals consist of one course and maybe something sweet, unless we eat out, when we might have an entrée as well. Or two entrées and skip the main. See what I mean? Even for those of us who make a living writing about wine and food, dinner at home is usually a bowl of pasta and a salad, or a take-away curry, or pie and chips, just like everybody else.

Well it is for me, anyway, and, like everybody else, I've usually got only one bottle on the table. The remains of last night's riesling perhaps, or a half-empty bottle of shiraz that's been sitting around since the barbecue at the weekend but still tastes okay (if not better than it did when first opened). Whatever wine comes to hand. That's how I discovered that rich oaky chardonnay is delicious with grilled lamb chops: I would normally have opted for a cabernet (the classic match), but happened to have a bottle of chardonnay open in the fridge, so gave it a go.

Some matches of wine and food work better than others, and common sense comes into it again. If I had half a dozen oysters in front of me and the only bottle in the house was a big, tannic shiraz, I'd probably opt for a glass of water rather than pull the cork. Or go hungry and drink the shiraz. On the other hand, if somebody served up a venison pie and the only bottle around was a young, pale chenin blanc — which would have been perfect with the oysters — I'd wish I hadn't drunk the shiraz.

The suggestions and tips on the next few pages are ways of enjoying wine and food that work for me. They don't comprise a definitive list. They're just a start. The best I can hope for is that this bit of the book makes you want to get up and go out to a market, a bottle shop or a restaurant and try some good wine and food yourself.

Antipasto, Aperitif — Stimulate the Taste Buds

All meals have to start somewhere, and a pretty good way to start is by opening a bottle of something delicious and nibbling on something savoury.

The first thing you put in your mouth should make the taste buds come alive and leave them yearning for more excitement. So while you're roasting the capsicum and opening the oysters and putting the olives in a bowl and warming through the soup, a great thing to open would be a bottle of sparkling wine.

The delicate flavour and the tingling acid of good bubbly has worked for generations of people looking for something to stimulate their tongues, and it's always a safe bet as a starter. A young, crisp riesling or sauvignon blanc/ semillon blend is also a good way to liven up the palate, as is a bone-dry fino-style sherry — a wine which isn't usually much more alcoholic than a ripe sauvignon blanc anyway.

Sherry is a wine style that many people overlook when they're thinking about what to drink with a meal, and that's a shame, because often it's the best thing of all — especially with antipasto or tapas, or on its own as an aperitif. Open a Spanish manzanilla, with its character-istic nutty, salty tang and try it with a bowl of olives, some grilled sardines and crusty bread sprinkled with a fruity olive oil and you'll see what I mean. Or try a slightly fuller-flavoured amontillado sherry with a clear, Thai-influenced crab consommé, the heady ginger, garlic and chilli flavour of the soup mingling with the grilled nuts character of the wine. Sherry is classically partnered with soup, and is also making a new reputation for itself in combination with a few Asian cuisines.

And this won't be the first time you'll read this, but don't forget rosé. A couple of years ago I might not have been so enthusiastic, but quite a few winemakers are having another go at this

Food and wine matching is pretty simple stuff really. There are no complicated chemical equations or golden rules to memorise. Only common sense.

neglected style and coming up with some delicious wines. Drunk really cold on a really hot day, rosé might not have the tastebud-wake-up-call crispness we're after, but it's often just the thing for a big plateful of antipasto.

Vegies, Salads — Match Flavours

Think green. Think of a cool bowl full of fresh-picked rocket and baby spinach leaves, each leaf gleaming with olive oil and balsamic vinegar, tossed with a finely chopped assortment of fresh herbs, and sprinkled with crumbly pale parmesan. Think of a perfect big tomato, sunshine-warm from the plant, sliced into thick juicy rounds and topped with bold green basil leaves. Think of chunky slices of eggplant, zucchini and green pepper, piled on a plate, streaked black from the grill and dusted with cracked pepper. And think of fresh whole-grain bread, still warm from the oven, pulled apart into hand-sized pieces.

Almost any cold white wine you could think of would be good with a lunch like that, but for me, sauvignon blanc just has the edge as the ultimate vegie-and-salad wine. Whether it's the asparagus and green pea flavours you can find in sauvignon blanc from New Zealand or the nettles and fresh-cut grass in Sancerre, from France's Loire Valley, there's an undeniable greenness to sauvignon blanc — and sauvignon/semillon blends — which seems to say 'drink me with vegetables'.

One of the best ways to think about food and wine is to think about matching flavours. That's why I mostly like sauvignon blanc with vegies. It's why I like something a little fuller like lightly-wooded chardonnay with a fuller-flavoured salad, say a niçoise, with tuna and anchovies and olives. And why, if those grilled vegies I mentioned have been marinated in a garlic-infused oil, a young, fruity grenache rosé is perfect with them (grenache and garlic are great flavour partners).

If you're going to pile your salad high with goodies like roast duck or quail then you might as well forget white wine, and crack open a bottle of pinot noir or sparkling red. The gamey flavours in these wines will go well with the flavour in the game ingredients.

Food and wine matching is pretty simple stuff really. There are no complicated chemical equations or golden rules to memorise. Only common sense. In this case, put light-flavoured wines with light-flavoured vegies, and fuller, more robust wines with vegetables — or other ingredients — that have fuller, more robust flavours. Easy.

Snacks and Savouries — Simple Flavours, Simple Wines

Not every meal can be a gastronomic extravaganza, with an array of brilliantly composed and perfectly executed dishes cunningly matched with various subtle and multi-faceted wines. Much as I would love it to be like that, life is just too short (and I'm already far too plump for my own good).

But then neither food nor wine have to be complex or expensive to be lip-smackingly, soul-hearteningly, deeply, deeply enjoyable. In fact, sometimes the simplest flavours can be the best.

A plate of oysters and a glass of clean, fresh, even quite neutral white. A pigeon pie and a glass of pinot noir. A hearty southern French red, a hunk of mature cheese, a crust of bread and a peaceful spring afternoon to sleep it off and I'm in heaven.

There are a few simple, flavoursome, not particularly complicated (and not very expensive) wines that are reliably easy-going with a huge range of flavours. Cheap bubbly, light whites like pinot grigio and chenin blanc, good beaujolais or light pinot noir, cheaper Italian reds like young chianti or dolcetto, and fruity whites like young marsanne or simple riesling are all great stand-by wines, wines to pull out at an impromptu barbecue, or Saturday afternoon picnic, or trip to the beach, or even just when you feel like a snack and a glass of something nice.

Spice — Break all the Rules

Never believe anyone who tells you that certain foods don't go with wine — until you've tried them for yourself. Artichokes and chocolate, for example, are traditionally regarded as wine-unfriendly, but with a little imagination even they can be made to succumb. Grill the artichokes, marinate them in olive oil and herbs and chuck them on a pizza with lots of cheese and tomatoes, pull out a bottle of feisty Italian red and I doubt anyone will complain. Serve the richest chocolate cake you can make with a bottle of the richest Rutherglen tokay you can buy and I *guarantee* no-one will complain.

The best reason for not drinking a certain wine with certain foods is personal preference. For example, there's nothing in fish and chips that clashes with, say, a light unwooded chardonnay — in fact the two could have been made for each other. But years of (extensive) research have led me to the firm opinion that I'd *much* rather have a cold beer instead.

And then there is chilli. And ginger, and garlic and lemon grass and Vietnamese mint and the dozens of spices that are used in the increasingly popular styles of cookery loosely huddled under the 'Asian' banner (not to mention the spicy food of the Middle East, Africa, South America . . .)

As long as the food is not so overpoweringly hot that it knocks your taste buds for six, spices and even chilli aren't things to be afraid of when it comes to drinking wine. And the huge diversity of spicy foods available certainly deserves a little more vinous respect and imagination than the traditional recommendation of medium-sweet gewürztraminer.

Having said that, though, gewürztraminer — and its aromatic cousin, riesling — can be brilliant wines to have with spicy foods. There's something about the wonderful fragrance of much Thai food, for example, that goes well with the wonderful fragrance of a very young and dry but fruity gewürztraminer from Alsace in France or New Zealand or the cooler parts of Australia. And the intense, almost sweet-and-sour flavours of an older South Australian riesling can be delicious with the ginger, garlic and soy of some Chinese food.

But step outside the relatively safe bet of aromatic whites and you can come across some really exciting new combinations. Chilli, in moderation, and in conjunction with the sweetness of soy and the perfume of coriander in Indonesian or Malay cooking, can be great with a full, supple, velvety pinot noir. The fiery, dusty spices of Moroccan cooking could have

been made for big, spicy alcoholic blends of shiraz and grenache. The delicate, precise flavours of tempura or the softer, earthier flavours of miso soup are perfect with the earthy, nutty flavours of sherries, both dry and sweeter. And the salads, seafood and vegetables of Vietnamese food are tremendous with crisp, dry, grassy sauvignon blanc and semillon.

Experiment with your favourite wines and your favourite spicy foods. They may well not go together all the time — and might often clash — but occasionally you will come across a flavour combination that just dances on your tongue.

Fish — Weigh up the Alternatives

One of the best ways to put food and wine together is to think about the 'weight' of the food you want to eat and the 'weight' of the wine you want to drink. Think about how light, middleweight or heavy the food is in terms of flavour, texture and richness, and try to match it with a wine which is similarly light-, medium- or full-bodied.

Just think for a moment about fish. The classic fish-with-white-wine recommendation, while a reliable generalisation, is distinctly lacking in detail when you consider how many thousands of different types of fish there are in the sea (and the rivers, the streams, the dams and the estuaries). But apply the idea about 'weight' and the picture becomes a little clearer.

Imagine a simple, perfectly grilled fillet of King George whiting on your plate, perhaps sprinkled with a little lemon juice and black pepper. Now this light fish, delicate and gently

Now picture your plate groaning with a heavy barbecued cutlet of fleshy Blue Eye cod, glistening with an olive-oil-and-herb marinade. The riesling would be a fine match — but that rich, oaky chardonnay would be much better.

Seafood such as oysters, prawns, scallops, mussels and octopus all have clean, sea-fresh flavours that go well with clean, tangy wines. Oily fish such as sardines, pilchards and garfish benefit from being drunk with really crisp, unwooded whites, too — wines with good acidity to cut through the oiliness. The cool, slightly fuller impact of smoked fish like salmon and trout goes well with the slightly fuller impact of sparkling wine or lightly-wooded whites. Soft-textured but quite rich white fish like dory, hapuka and gemfish, and the sometimes substantial flavour of crayfish and yabbies, are all perfect partners for soft and rich whites like wooded chardonnay or older semillon.

Wooded whites are also good with the meatier, fleshier fish such as Atlantic salmon cutlets, tuna steaks and swordfish, but you might also want to think about trying supple, low-tannin lighter reds too, such as young pinot noir.

Yes. Red wine with fish. It's delicious.

Meat — It all Depends on the Cooking, but . . .

Right. I've talked about matching flavours, and breaking the rules, and matching weight for weight. Now I'm going to throw the vinous cat among the gastronomic pigeons and say that when it comes to putting food and wine

Yes. Red wine with fish. It's delicious.

cooked, might be overpowered by a heavy wine (like a rich, oak-matured chardonnay), whereas a light wine — a crisp, dry, steely riesling, say, or a good Italian soave — would complement the 'weight' of the food perfectly.

together, everything *really* depends on how the food has been cooked. And this applies to meat more than any other food.

Take chicken. In fact, take *a* chicken, one that's free-range, corn-fed, plump, fresh and succulent. Now take the breast fillets and poach gently in vegetable stock, cool, slice and serve with salad greens; take the wings and legs, marinate in olive oil and garlic and barbecue; and take what is left and stew very slowly in red wine with plenty of aromatic vegetables and herbs and red wine.

Even though it's exactly the same bird being cooked, different wines would work better with each of the differently cooked dishes. A riesling or other light, fruity white would be great with the poached breast; the oaky, toasty flavours of a wooded chardonnay or a young pinot noir would be perfect for the smoky flavours of the barbecued chook; and a hearty southern French red, or an older shiraz, would be good with the hearty, winey, wintry broth.

So even though there *are* general guides as to which wines go well with which meat, always think about how that meat is being cooked and the other ingredients that will go with it.

The classic simplicity of meat dishes like a roast rack of lamb or the Sunday joint of beef both cry out for the classic partner of a fine, sturdy cabernet sauvignon. But cover the lamb in Middle Eastern spices and serve with couscous and I'd veer towards a spicy, grenache-based wine from southern France, or a robust zinfandel. And slice the beef into strips and stir fry for a warm Thai salad and I'd look to a very good, richly fruity pinot noir for help in washing it down.

Pinot noir is also the first avenue I go down when confronted by anything remotely gamey (like duck, rabbit, squab or quail), or offaly (like liver), because of its earthy, slightly gamey flavours. Either pinot or something equally sensual and autumnal, like a good older shiraz. But at the same time Peking duck seems to have this bizarre but brilliant affinity for rich sparkling reds, and some rabbit and quail dishes are so light that you wouldn't want to drink anything heavier than a light semillon.

Remember, too, that many well-established food and wine matches began life as regional specialities: the peculiar brilliance of Alsace riesling with the local pork charcuterie; the truffle-like scent of Piemontese nebbiolo and the truffle-strewn roasts of Piemonte; the boeuf bourguignon of Burgundy with a good, rich, red burgundy.

Now while Australia has few food and wine matches that can truly be described as regional specialities — existing in, or solely originating from one place — that doesn't stop us gleefully and successfully putting local food and wine together whenever we can, or from emulating the classic combinations of Europe and elsewhere.

It makes sense, for example, to serve a McLaren Vale grown and made sangiovese wine with McLaren Vale reared veal stewed with McLaren Vale olives and McLaren Vale bread drizzled with McLaren Vale olive oil, even if we are thousands of miles from Tuscany, where such a match originated. It makes sense to match Tasmanian oysters with Tasmanian sparkling wine. And it makes absolute sense to drink warm and rich Barossa shiraz with the wonderfully big flavour of South Australian kangaroo.

Cheese — Textures
(and Personal Preference)

Ah, cheese. How many parties/functions/
openings/meetings have you been to where
some rough old red is being handed round in
plastic cups, accompanied by paper plates
piled high with little cubes of yellow stuff
masquerading as cheddar? Well the good
news is that there is more to cheese and wine
(and life) than that.

Unlike the other foods that I've been raving
on about, cheeses are fairly easy to recommend
wine matches with because they so clearly fall
into different types. Soft cheese is soft cheese,
and hard cheese is hard cheese, and never the
twain shall meet. In fact, the only problem here
is the only real problem with any of these

recommendations: personal preference. I might
think a really pungent sauvignon blanc with a
spanking fresh goat's cheese is a flavour combination made in gastroheaven, but you might
think it tastes disgusting.

That goat's cheese is a good place to start.
Fresh, only-days-old cheeses like this, soft, still
milky and with simple, direct flavours, are
usually best with wines that also have simple,
direct flavours (which is why I like sauvignon
blanc, but bright young reds, really crisp young
sparklings and even really fruity rosés work
equally well). Soft cheeses that have also got
a white mould on them — aged goat, brie,
camembert — need a wine with a bit more
oomph, such as a wood-aged white, a more
robust, vintage bubbly, a soft pinot noir, or a
young merlot.

Washed-rind cheeses, with their sometimes
offputtingly stinky character and full-on barnyardy flavour, need a wine that will match them
head on: something with really aromatic, positive fruit like a shiraz, or a really barnyardy,
gamey pinot noir.

Hard cheeses — a group which includes
a host of cheeses from tangy cheddar to
bouncy gruyère to intense parmigiano reggiano
— is where you get to bring out your big reds.
It's the firm texture and bite of a good farm-
house cheddar that makes it go so well with
the firm structure of a young cabernet sauvignon, and the crumbly, almost grainy texture
of a good reggiano that makes it go so well with
the almost grainy tannins of an older shiraz
or sangiovese or the effervescence of a sparkling red.

And then there is blue. When it comes to
drinking something with blue cheese, especially

really pongy, in-your-face, no-holds-barred blue, those vintage port-swilling red-nosed major generals (with gout) had the right idea. You need a wine that is going to be able to stand up to the immense flavour attack of good blue cheese — and vintage port, really intense dessert wines like botrytis semillon, and liqueur muscat and tokay have just what it takes.

But all that, of course, is just my opinion.

Desserts — and to Finish

Still got some room left after all that? Just a small space in the corner of your belly? Good. Because this is where we get a bit indulgent, and forget about diets, dentists and the next morning.

What would life be without pudding? The final sweet flourish at the end of a meal — whether it's a simple bowl of fruit or a carefully constructed sugary extravagance — is the bit that should send you to your bed (or off out to party, or whatever) with fond, warm memories and a distinct glow. And the wine can play a crucial part in that.

Matching wine to desserts is relatively simple. There are really only two things to remember.

The first is to drink a wine that is at least as sweet — if not sweeter — than what you are eating, or the wine will be overpowered by the food. For example, a perfect pear, or other unadorned fruit would be good with something not too sweet, like a late harvest riesling. But slice the pear thinly and bake it in a tart, covered in caramelised syrup, and you'll need a much sweeter, botrytis-affected riesling to stand up to it.

All the other considerations hold true, too — the matching of flavours (anything involving apricot and/or butterscotch is particularly good with the apricot flavours in botrytis-affected semillon), textures (the citrus tang of a lemon tart and the crisp acid of an ice wine) and weight (a slab of cake needs a fortified dessert wine with slabs of flavour and alcohol to do it justice) — but the point about sweetness is probably the most useful.

The other thing to remember is that (as far as I'm concerned) wine and ice-cream or sorbets just don't mix. The intense cold tends to numb your tongue and make wine feel like it isn't even in your mouth. But then again, as I said, never believe anyone who tells you that certain foods don't go with wine until you've tried them for yourself.

Blood
Health and wine

'Hold on, doctor. Run that one by me again. You're saying that a couple of glasses of red wine a day could stop me having a heart attack?'

'Yes, but it's not quite as simple as that, Ms . . .'

'You beauty! So I can eat rich foods and live a lazy life, just like those fat peasants in the South of France do, and because I'm also knocking back the old vino, it stops me keeling over and croaking!'

'Sort of, but . . .'

'That's it. I'm off. Thanks, doc. You've made me feel a whole lot better already. Hey, listen: where's the nearest bottle shop?'

'I . . .'

Modern science, in all its wisdom, has, in the last ten years or so, repeatedly thrilled the world with report after report, study after study, each claiming to prove that the moderate consumption of alcohol — particularly wine, and particularly red wine — can actually be good for you.

As the world listened in amazement, researcher after researcher told us that we could reduce the risk of a heart attack through sensible imbibing. It was the best news we (and the wine trade) had had since bronze-age humans discovered the wonders of fermentation.

But it's not really news, is it? I mean it's just scientific 'proof' of something that civilisation — and even science itself, in its heart — has known for as long as we've been making and drinking wine: that the stuff is good for you. Apart from anything else, it's common sense.

You get home from a hard day and pour yourself a cool glass of your favourite chardonnay. It makes you feel better. See what I mean? Common sense. Do we really need scientists to show us cold hard evidence of what we already know?

getting any better. And despite the fact that it accounts for a relatively small proportion of these problems (compared to beer and spirits), wine is still cast as one of the major demons

So what exactly is moderation? For some it's 'a glass now and again', for others, it's 'not enough to make me fall over, but just enough to make me happy'. But they're hardly reliable scientific guidelines, are they?

Well yes, we do. Because we've lost the trust in wine that previous generations had.

The very first doctors knew that there are substances in wine that have definite positive effects on the human body — not least of which is alcohol, an effective anaesthetic. Wine was an essential medicine for the ancient Greeks and Romans, and particular types of wine were prescribed for patients suffering from all sorts of ailments until relatively recently.

Then, towards the end of the nineteenth century, the temperance (later prohibition) movement waged war against the demon drink that was apparently ruining society, and wine's widespread medicinal use (and widespread enjoyment) was curtailed.

In the twenty-first century, alcohol's image in society is just as tarnished. Over-indulgence, under-age binge drinking; families ruined by alcoholism; deaths from drink driving — these are very real concerns for communities all over the world, and they don't seem to be

responsible for society's breakdown.

It was against such a background of neo-prohibitionism in the United States that the recent research came out, and that's why everybody made so much noise about it. We pounced on these hard facts showing wine in a positive light. Medical wisdom, for once, had come down on the side of enjoying yourself.

What the most widely reported research claimed — and it was extensive research, involving thousands of case studies done over decades — was that the moderate consumption of red wine can help prevent heart disease. The phenolics in the wine (the pigment, the tannins) have the effect of lowering the amount of cholesterol deposited in our arteries, reducing the risk of clots and blockages — and therefore of cardiovascular diseases like heart attack and stroke. This was called the French Paradox, because it was most noticeable in south-west France, where the inhabitants eat copious amounts of saturated fats and drink lots of red wine, yet have very low rates of heart disease.

But wait, there's more. Other research showed that moderate wine drinking can also lower blood pressure, make you more alert and intelligent as you get older, raise morale, act as an appetite stimulant, a relaxant and an aid to digestion. And not only that, but wine in moderation is also very much recommended as an essential part of the Mediterranean diet: plenty of cereals and grain, lots of vegies, non-saturated fats such as olive oil, and a little meat and dairy.

None of which would have surprised the original Mediterraneans, the ancient Greeks and Romans, in the slightest.

Moderation

So what exactly *is* moderation? For some it's 'a glass now and again', for others, it's 'not enough to make me fall over, but just enough to make me happy'. But they're hardly reliable scientific guidelines, are they?

The question of moderation is one that medical authorities and governments have been wrestling with for decades, and the answer they have come up with is based on the 'standard drink', or 'unit of alcohol'.

A standard drink is measured as ten grams of alcohol in Australia, and eight grams of alcohol in the UK. That, very roughly, equates to a small glass of wine, a very small glass of fortified, a shot of spirits or a glass of beer. The recommended limits for moderate consumption in Australia are four standard drinks a day for men, and two for women — based on the different ways alcohol is handled by the male and female body. And it's expressed like this — four and two a day rather than twenty-eight and fourteen a week — because it is better to have a regular, moderate intake rather than knock back your weekly dose in one hit.

Now that would all be fine and dandy if we were 'standard' humans. But we're not. We're fat and thin, tall and short, at the peak of physical fitness and in the trough of couch potato-ism. We're young, we're old, we're healthy, we're ill, we're pregnant, we're stressed, we're relaxed. So, yet again, common sense must prevail, using the recommendations as a starting point.

The good news is that, whether you're a big and healthy young man enjoying four glasses of wine a day, or a healthy pregnant woman enjoying one or two glasses a week, you are not only probably drinking in moderation, but may even live longer because of it.

Globe

The changing world of wine

It all used to be so easy. In the good old days, that is, when our parents began to drink wine. Whether you were growing up in Sydney, San Francisco or London, nobody knew or cared about the names of grape varieties, or whether a wine had been through partial malolactic, or whether the Heat Degree Day summation of the climate of Oregon was similar to that of Burgundy. Our parents just drank pretty much what their parents drank – rough reds and flabby whites with generic names like burgundy and moselle and the occasional glass of champagne.

Today, as the last light of the twentieth century fades from the horizon, things are nowhere near as easy — but they're much more exciting. The world of wine, just like the rest of the world, has changed beyond recognition over the last thirty years. We're drinking better wines, more interesting wines, and we are

bombarded with more information about these wines than we could ever possibly hope to need.

Today, if you're growing up in Sydney or San Francisco, the wines on the good bottle-shop shelves and in the good restaurants are as likely to come from a small vineyard just outside the city as they are from a small vineyard in Bordeaux or Italy or South America. And in London there is a whole generation of people who hardly ever drink what their parents drank, but are learning a lot about wine through the Australian and Californian bottles that crowd their wine-shop shelves.

There's a convenient way of describing the situation the wine world is in at the beginning of the twenty-first century, and that's to split it into two: the Old World and the New World.

The Old World — Europe — is where the models for the well-known wine styles were developed, in regions that often gave their name to the styles. In Burgundy they make burgundy, in Champagne they make champagne, using techniques passed down from generation to generation, with methods of growing grapes and making wine enshrined in law. The Old World is slow to change, doesn't readily respond to fluctuations in the market, and uses centuries of tradition as an excuse. Producers in the Old World are convinced they are making the best wines on the planet.

The New World — everybody else (Australasia, the Americas, South Africa) — is where the well-known wine styles are refashioned in sometimes completely different images. In California they make pinot noir, in Australia they make sparkling wine, using high-tech equipment and the latest innovative winemaking techniques, with very little about what they do enshrined in law. The New World is quick to change, responds perhaps too readily to market demands and sees having no burdensome traditions as one of its greatest assets. Producers in the New World are convinced they are making the best wines on the planet.

Of course, in reality things are a little less cut and dried. Old World/New World is more about ways of thinking than actual physicality. Some of the most exciting New World developments, for instance, are actually taking place in the vineyards of the Old, just as Old World ways of thinking are being rediscovered among the vineyards of the New.

During the 1980s, Australian and Australian-trained wine-makers flew in to the south of France, Hungary and former Soviet countries and elsewhere, applied their techniques and turned previously atrocious wine into perfectly drinkable wine. And the 1990s saw a growing new tradition among local winemakers in staunchly traditional countries such as Italy of rebelling against the prevailing outdated system, and producing the wines they want, where they want, how they want.

Likewise, in the New World, many winemakers are picking through the bones of Old World wisdom and applying it successfully in a new context: each year, more and more winemakers are willing to admit that there might be something in the old French gobbledegook after all, and fewer are relying solely on technology to make their wine, preferring instead to use more 'natural', traditional techniques.

You could argue that the biggest development in the so-called New World, though, has been the increasing focus on regional identity.

'Regionalism' is the new buzzword: the acknowledgement that certain grape varieties do better in certain areas, and that this is something worth promoting. Regionalism has led to a revival of interest in 'traditional' New World wine styles (big, alcoholic shiraz and grenache from the Barossa and McLaren Vale in Australia, for example, or equally big, old vine zinfandel from California) and a surge of interest in 'new' regional wine styles (Marlborough sauvignon blanc, Washington state merlot).

This is, of course, precisely the kind of terroir-driven argument that the Old World has been developing for centuries.

But what of the future? Well, the world of wine appears to have been moving in two directions for a while now, and shows little sign of slowing down or changing course.

On the one hand, the big wine companies are growing in size; while, on the other hand, the small, independent, struggling family wineries are growing in number. Either way, the vineyard expansion in key New World wine countries such as the US and Australia is simply staggering.

On the one hand, you have the larger producers and more budget-conscious consumers searching for affordable 'international' styles such as peachy chardonnay and blackcurranty cabernet, regardless of where they're made — resulting in a sea of good-value, clean and fruity wines that is being lapped up by new drinkers across the world.

On the other hand (and more than partly as a reaction to the first movement), a growing band of usually smaller winemakers is focussing on obscure and indigenous grape varieties and techniques to affirm their sense of place and individuality — and a growing band of usually more quality-conscious drinkers is supporting these more individual wines.

And while technology in both vineyard and winery is undoubtedly helping us produce some of the cleanest, most exciting, best value wines we've ever tasted, a very real concern about the environmental impact of the industry is forcing a rethink about that technological intervention, and a return to more gentle, sustainable, traditional methods of grape growing and winemaking.

Of course, what all this means in the short and perhaps even long term is that we can look forward to drinking a wider range of even better wines. And that, at the end of the day, is really something to live for.

Acknowledgements

Sophie & Bridie for being patient; Adair for being understanding; Sue Hines for having faith in the idea in the first place; Tracy O'Shaughnessy for keeping us on the right track; Andrew Cunningham and Luisa Liano for making it look so good; Jim and Phillipa, Geoff, Nigel, Dave, Michael and Lois at Wandin Valley Estate for letting us run around their winery and vineyard, for giving us the silver shed port and for being models; Growlers for having such groovy water bottles; Caroline Evans for assisting (with the camera gear and the polishing off of the silver shed port); Ned, Tim Bell, John Short, Lindsey Edwards and Scott Wright for assisting too and being good about missing out on the silver shed port; the Big Men in Tights at Bloodwood for being so deliciously pink; Peter Curtis at the Hunter Valley Cheese Company for the time in the cool room and the wellies; the old shiraz vine at Tyrrell's for still being there; the Draytons for an interesting bottling line; Stumpy the Frogmouth for spooking us out; N. and A.L. Phillips for the water tank, the vineyard and Sam the dog; the Irelands at Peppers Creek for their winery; Ponch Hawkes for equipment and studio time; Lab X for doing a good quick job with processing; David and Jane Lowe and Gemma Funnell for red winemaking; Barry and Jan Shields at Oakvale for the basket press; the Hallidays for encouragement; Ross Bird for making us look like rock stars; Gerald Diffey for letting Max experiment on his staff; Creina Stockley at the AWRI, Jeffrey Grosset in the Clare and Steven Strachan at the WFA for some facts and figures; Richard Piper for inadvertantly opening the door; the sceptical winemakers and amused riddlers at Domaine Chandon; Megan at the Builders Arms for the bar and cocktails; Tim de Neefe and Peter Mack for help with equipment; Michael Hoyle and all at Eyton on Yarra for for letting us get under their feet in the kitchen and cellar door; Jeremy Strode and Simon Denton at the Adelphi for space and pudding and trays of meat; Fiona Hammond for a bit of food styling; Jason, Eugenie, Rick, Annabel, Paul N., Millie and Murray for standing around; Dan and The Becmeister for some equipment; Rob Evans at McCoppins for the till and the fridge; Langton's Auctions for the cellar stuff; Richard Thomas at the Yarra Valley Dairy for yet more cheese; Stephanie Wood at The Age Epicure Uncorked for some pics; everybody else who helped and who we've forgotten; but most of all, credit must be given to the legendary silver shed port, which gave us more than a little inspiration and more than enough thick heads.

Max Allen would also like to acknowledge the following for inspiring certain parts of this book: George Orwell's 'The Moon under Water' an article on the ideal pub, originally published in the *Evening Standard* in 1946 and reprinted in *The Faber Book of Drink, Drinkers and Drinking*, which inspired the wine shop in the chapter Cash; and Oliver Mayo's gloriously evocative description of a vine pruner at work in his book *The Wines of Australia* which inspired the rain-drenched old man featured in the chapter Sun.

Index

acid 57, 101
age 102, 121–5
appellation 101
auctions 114

barbera 23
barrels 59, 68, 102
basket press 61, 102
blending 7–9, 10, 13, 15, 19, 57, 68, 80
botrytis-affected white wine 73
Botrytis cinerea 71, 102, 122
breathing, importance of 127–9

cabernet family 18–20
cabernet franc 19
cabernet sauvignon 18–19, 141
carbonic maceration 67
carignan 24
cask wine 10, 15
cellar door sales 113–14
cellaring 117–18
chaptalisation 57, 103
characteristics 101–9
chardonnay 5–6, 10, 57, 80
cheese and wine 141–3
chenin blanc 11–12
cinsaut 24
climate, effect on grapes 12, 27–8
clubs 114
colombard 12
Côte-Rôtie 21

decanting 103, 128–9
desserts and wine 143
dolcetto 22
doradillo (grape) 15
durif 23

extended maceration 68

fermentation 56, 58, 59, 61, 66, 67, 105
fining and filtering 69, 105
food and wine 11–12, 115, 133–43
fortified wines
    madeira 86
    making 83–7
    muscat 14–15, 87
    master recipe 84
    port
    tawny 87
    vintage 86–7

serving suggestions 87
sherry 15, 84–6, 135
solera system 86
styles 84–7
tokay 15, 87

gamay 23
glossary 99–109
gewürztraminer 11
grenache 21–2

harvesting 43–4
    late 71, 75
health and wine 145–7
Hermitage 21

Italian wine 22–3

late harvest white wine 72
liqueur muscat 84, 87

madeira 86
mail order 114
malbec 20
malolactic fermentation 59, 107
marsanne 13–14, 56
mataro 22
merlot 19–20
mould 71–5
mourvèdre 22
muscadelle 15
muscat 14–15, 84, 87

nebbiolo 22

palomino (grape) 15
pedro ximinez (grape) 15
petit verdot 20
pinot gris 12
pinot meunier 24, 80
pinot noir 17–18, 67, 68, 80, 141
port
    tawny 87
    vintage 23–4, 86–7

red grapes
    barbera 23
    cabernet family 18–20
    cabernet franc 19
    cabernet sauvignon 18–19
    carignan 24

cinsaut 24
dolcetto 22
durif 23
gamay 23
grenache 21–2
Italian 22–3
malbec 20
mataro 22
merlot 19–20
mourvèdre 22
nebbiolo 22
petit verdot 20
pinot meunier 24
pinot noir 17–18
sangiovese 23
shiraz 20–1
tempranillo 24
touriga 23–4
zinfandel 23
red wine
    barrels 68
    blending 19, 21, 68
    carbonic maceration 67
    extended maceration 68
    fermenting 61, 66, 67
    fining and filtering 69, 105
    making 61–9
    older 123–5
    plunging, turning, pumping over 67–8
    pressings 68
    serving suggestions 66, 128
    wild yeasts 67
    whole-bunch fermentation or stalk
        return 67
riesling 10–11, 56
restaurants 115
Rhône Valley 12–13, 21
rosé 62
roussanne 13–14

sangiovese 23
sauvignon blanc 6–9
seafood and wine 11–12, 138–9
seasons, effect on grapes 39–41
semillon 7, 9–10, 56
serving
    and decanting 128–9
    fortified wine 87
    red wine 66, 128
    sparkling wine 79
    temperature 127–8